The Cosmology of Not
&
the Landscape of Being

Written by

Thomas Vaughn

The Cosmology of Not
&
The Landscape of Being

By
Thomas Vaughn

ISBN: 978-1-7372750-3-9

For information about permission to reproduce selections
from this book, send email to
reproductions@notfoundation.com

For more information on the Cosmology of Not or the
Landscape of Being, send inquiries to
inquiries@notfoundation.com

Cover art and book design
by Thomas Vaughn

CMOS-LOB_2024_0209_1313

Contents

THE BEFORE

As I talk about the Cosmology of Not in this work, I do so with three major themes in mind: the evolution of the Self, the evolution of humanity, and the evolution of the universe.

EVOLUTION OF THE SELF

When I think about *my* Self, I think about not just *who* I am now, but also who I *have been* in the past. I think about the journey I have taken to get to where I am today. I have made many mistakes. I have helped people, but I have also hurt many people, including myself. It's hard to imagine, though, what I would do if I could do it over again. I'm not sure I would want that opportunity. Today, I love who I am and who I am still becoming. I still battle some demons and I still have to grapple with the Adversary of Self[1] at times, but I have also found a loving guide in the Self – in *my* Self – to help me.

But there was an evolution to this Self. Just like you, the path I have walked to get here goes all the way back to my teenage years, my childhood years, my toddler years and keeps going back to when I was a baby, a fetus, embryo, zygote and even further back to the time I was just an idea of warm, light, active presence.

Our discussion of the Self in this work will begin before the Self was even a dream of *being,* and we will move up from there into the Landscape of Being where each living Self is today, working, eating, sleeping, paying bills, and trying to make it through day-to-day life.

---

[1] We can be our own worst enemies. (But we can also be one of our best friends).

This evolution of the Self we can also call the Cosmology of the Self.

EVOLUTION OF HUMANITY

Humanity shares a similar history to that of a Self. Humanity can trace its "Self" back in time to when humans did not realize that stars were actually suns. Further back, we find a time when humans thought that the forces of nature were supernatural beings we now call angles, demons, and gods. Further back in time, there was a time we could not even write. During this ancient time, we passed down information from one generation to the next using songs and stories. Even further back in time we were nomadic hunter-gathering animals wandering the forests and the plains in search of food. Even further back in time humanity was a handful of unrecognizable mammalian creatures who were not even self-aware. Further back still, we were some kind of creatures who had just learned how to leave the sea and walk on dry land. Go back further and we were tiny primitive sea creatures. Before this, just like the Self, humanity, as "life itself," was an idea of warm, light, active presence.

As we trace the Cosmology of Not, from the beginning to the now, we will trace it along the lines of human evolution – from warm, light, active presence to the people we are now, moving around and interacting with each other across the Landscape of Being.

EVOLUTION OF THE UNIVERSE

Finally, there is the universe we all find ourselves expanding with. The universe is everything around us, panning out into space for trillions and zillions of miles until all we see is hundreds of billions of galaxies all spinning around in some kind of cosmic dance that none of us can fully see from our vantage point on this little planet we call Earth.

The universe, like humanity and the Self, also has a past. Going backward in time, we imagine that billions of years ago the galaxies were just beginning to form. Before the galaxies formed there were incomprehensible amounts of matter and energy swirling around with space itself as it was all expanding "outward." Looking further back in time we see this expansion outward was the result of some kind of unfathomably massive explosion of primordial energy. Looking even further back from this instantaneous explosion, we imagine the universe was a quantum singularity. Even further back before the quantum singularity, beneath the superstring, like humanity and the Self, we find the universe was an idea of warm, light, active presence.

I really have to go all the way back to before the beginning of the Self, humanity, and the universe in order to explain the Cosmology of Not. The reason for starting before the beginning will make much more sense after I explain what Not is.

Before we dive into Not, though, I feel it is important to introduce myself and provide a bit of a framework for how my search for Self, led to Not.

SPIRITUAL AWAKENING

When I was fourteen, I experienced what I later came to regard as my spiritual awakening. I was walking home from middle school in a suburban neighborhood in mid-Missouri, on a sunny afternoon in spring. Up until the moment of my awakening there was nothing particularly unusual about this day that could make it stand out from any other day. As I walked and my gaze wandered, it fell upon one of the houses

I was walking by. I stopped in my tracks and stared because I was suddenly stunned by what I saw. It is difficult to describe because with what I saw there was also a feeling that words can only meekly convey.

Visually, the house seemed to be emanating waves of energy. Much like a pebble in a pool, with the house being the pebble and the air around it being the pool. Wave after wave of "house energy" rippled out in every direction. The house itself, even though it seemed to be the source of the "house energy waves," looked like what I can only describe as "the most fragile of illusions." I looked at the small bright green shrub next to the house and it too was emanating energy. In this case it was "shrub energy," rippling outward and mixing with the house ripples, the two energies merging to create interference patterns in the air. The car in the driveway was rippling waves of "car energy." Everything I beheld was rippling with energy and these ripples were all merging with each other into the air and sky. Each of these rippling things in the world also had a characteristic of seeming to be illusory.

Returning my attention to the house, the illusion – which was the house itself – seemed so fragile that it seemed it could just blink out of existence at any moment. And at that moment, faster than the speed of thought, for the briefest instant, I had the impression that it did blink out and that I saw behind the veil of illusion. It was the most remarkable moment in my life. I was awestruck. But the glimpse I had was so brief that in the very instant that I saw it, I lost it. It was the beginning of the thought and feeling of, "This is the truth!" but only the beginning. It was a remarkable gift and a terrible curse. I felt I had seen a glimpse of the underpinnings of all of existence but not enough of a glimpse to be able to even ask what it was that I had seen.

The whole experience lasted around 60 to 90 seconds and then everything looked more or less just as it had before. I was dumbstruck as I looked around wishing that I could somehow recreate the experience. But I could not. I have never experienced anything like it since. In journaling throughout the years, I have referred to this moment as my spiritual birth, or my spiritual awakening, but it could also be described as the awakening (or the leveling-up) of my Spirit-Consciousness.

I continued to walk home but was left with a resounding question ringing through my entire being that can probably best be summed up by, "What is going on here?!" This question was easily reshaped as "What is the meaning of life?" Other questions quickly sprang forth: What is the point of human existence? What is this illusion all around us? Is there purpose here? If so, what is the purpose? What is behind it? Is there a big picture? What does the big picture look like? Where did this all come from? How did this come to be? What are we supposed to be doing? And so on and so on.

I started seeking answers diligently. I was more or less obsessed with finding answers. I asked anyone and everyone that was willing to talk about it. I sought answers through religion, philosophy, the esoteric, metaphysics, under rocks, behind trees, in the sky, in static on the television, through online bulletin boards (this was before the world wide web), in the thoughtful eyes of dogs and cats and even the seemingly knowing stare of little babies. I sought meaning from everything I beheld.

Nobody seemed to be able to explain any of it to me. Most people did not want to talk about it at all and some of the religious who *were* willing to talk would quickly become uncomfortable with my probing questions and would terminate the conversation with something to the effect of,

"You should talk to my preacher." In turn, when I did pursue the preachers, they would fairly quickly terminate the conversation with, "You should read the Bible." Or "You need to pray to Jesus. He will provide the answers you seek."

It is probably important that I stress just how intensely I sought answers. The desire to know what it was I had seen was burning inside me. So much so, that it literally hurt to not know. It was maddening.

About one year after my awakening, I experienced "getting high" for the first time. Marijuana and hallucinogenic drugs seemed to promise a doorway back to my experience of spiritual awakening, but they never quite delivered. I had some pretty incredible trips using hallucinogenic drugs over the next few years but none of them ever compared to my awakening experience.

By the age of 16 I had started drinking alcohol and smoking cigarettes. Being a drug-using, alcohol-drinking, cigarette-smoking teenager was something I embraced fully. I liked the image, but more than that I wanted to get back to my awakening again and there was another side-effect I discovered very helpful also. The more I partied, the more I was able to numb the burning curiosity which tortured my waking mind. Further, I was able to convince myself that getting stoned could somehow be interpreted as "work toward finding answers."

This incessant drive to find the answers was ever-present – like the constant hum of an engine on an endless road trip. I told myself and other people that I was "searching for myself," because those were some words I had picked up in some metaphysical literature. But I wasn't really searching for *myself*.

I was searching for answers that seemed much, much bigger than me.

I kept seeking the purpose of life. The best answers I could get from my parents, teachers or counselors was that I should graduate from high school, go to a trade school or college, get a degree, then get a job and climb the corporate ladder while I find a spouse and make little kids who I could then sentence to the same mindless infinite loop of copy/paste existence.

I saw the following pattern being offered to me:
Get up, go to work, come home, go to bed.
Get up, go to work, come home, go to bed.
Get up, go to work, come home, go to bed.

I was horrified by this prospect. I exclaimed, "Is that really all there is?! Does it really come down to this absurd endless cycle?"

I was awake and everyone else seemed to be sleepwalking.

I saw the pretense and façade that was society and I saw the sham that was money. Society and money were obviously pure illusion. I learned that money didn't even *really* exist. That money is an agreement between people to pretend that there is value in order to have a way to trade goods and services.

I refused to be a pawn in their system. Five months before graduation, I dropped out of high school and got my GED. I rejected the idea of college because I did not want to be a pawn in the absurd game of "Society," I felt was being pushed on me. I spent all of my free time partying while working unskilled labor jobs to make enough money to buy cigarettes, weed, alcohol, and other drugs (in that order).

After about three years of working jobs such as a fast-food worker, convenience store clerk, and warehouse worker, I had a startling epiphany.

My life had become an endless cycle of:
Get up, get high, go to work, come home, get high, go to bed.
Get up, get high, go to work, come home, get high, go to bed.
Get up, get high, go to work, come home, get high, go to bed.

It was then that I remembered that one of my biggest reasons for dropping out of high school was so that I could go "find myself." Honestly, I didn't really think that I was lost, but I had read a lot about "finding yourself" and just assumed I was lost because as a teenage dropout I knew I was supposed to be "lost." Looking back now, it makes sense that I did not really feel lost. After all, how can you be lost if you don't know where you're going?

But whether lost or found, I knew that the cycle I was enacting was not maximizing my potential as a human being and I felt guilt in allowing myself to walk this path of self-destruction. I was also completely perplexed that after having rejected the endless loop of day-to-day drudgery being pushed on me by parents, teachers, and society at large, I had nonetheless fallen victim to it anyway. How did this happen?!

At any rate, I knew it was wrong for me to slowly kill myself in this way. And I was painfully aware of the fact that I was definitely slowly killing myself.

To make a long story short, after a DWI resulting in a car wreck and many other disgraceful adventures then finally ending up being hospitalized due to a drunken fight, I ended up going into treatment for drug and alcohol abuse. After treatment, I went to college to get a degree in engineering and then over the course of the next twenty years I climbed the corporate ladder, got married and had two children whom my wife and I are now grooming for their run in the Machine.

This is life in the Landscape of Being. We all have to find our way through this landscape. We have to reconcile the idiotic meaninglessness of it all with the critical importance of it all.

As parents, my wife and I discuss this problem often and try to figure out solutions. How do we teach our children that the econociety they live in is an illusory and meaningless sham but that it is also critical that they take it seriously? Don't get me wrong – I am not saying that the beautiful treasure which is life is a meaningless sham. I'm talking about the paradigm humanity has created for ourselves that each of us has to adopt in order to make it through day-to-day existence. I'm talking about the "thank you, sir, may I have another" of it all.

After all, money *is* illusion, but if you don't pay your electric bill, the power company will turn off your electricity. Not having electricity might be an illusion too, but illusion or not, having no electricity makes cooking, watching TV and keeping yourself cool in the summer and warm in the winter extremely difficult.

It is here in the Landscape of Being that [insert some political party] claims it has the true and just view of the world and that all the other political parties are wrong. It is in the Landscape of Being that [insert some organized religion] announces that it is the only religion sanctioned by the only [insert god or gods] of the only universe and that all other gods and religions are false. It is here in the Landscape of Being that more than eight billion humans each point in a different direction and say, "That's the way we should be going."

The Landscape of Being is the world of day-to-day living. It is the slog (or the dance) through the mainstream[2] of society.

With its swirling masses of opposing but intermingling streams twisting in and out of the directionless mainstream it seems that the Landscape of Being is complete chaos. This is half true. True chaos is found in the Scattering of the warm, light, active presence of All, but we'll get to that later.

Here, in the Landscape of Being we have *the ordering* of chaos. But it is pockets of order mixed with pockets of chaos. In *The Mysteries*[3] I talk about how our fear of the unknown mixes with our lack of knowing what is going on in the universe to yield an insane lunacy which we all must coexist in. In short, what I argue is that deep down inside each and every one of us, we are terrified of the unknown. Add to this the fact that not a single human being knows what is going on here in this exploding cosmos we call "the universe." The result is chaotic and insanely deranged societies of humankind intermixing across the planet through the globalization afforded by advances in our own technology.

The powerful forces of economics, technology, politics, and religion are controlled by varying groups of people who have completely different ideas on what reality is and why we are here.[4]

---

[2] The "mainstream" being the swirling currents of mass-majority opinions on economics, media, entertainment, and politics.

[3] *The Mysteries: The equalizing power of knowing what we don't know*, Thomas Vaughn, 2023

[4] As in, "the purpose of life" for humans here on Earth.

Why can't we all agree on what reality looks like and what is most important to humanity?

I actually have a good answer for that question.

There is an old story that answers that question. It is the story of some blind monks and an elephant. I am going to reframe the story in modern terms to help explain why, when it comes to politics, half of the US population thinks they are right and thinks the other half of the US population is wrong. It does not matter which side of the political fence you are on – this story is the same for both sides.

Imagine a small, square building with four walls. One wall is made of steel, one of wood, one of glass and the other is plaster. Around the building are four blind people – one next to each of the four walls. The blind people are then asked to approach the thing in front of them and then explain to the world what they find.

The first one says, "It is a building made of steel."
The second one says, "It is a building made of wood."
The third one says, "It is a building made of glass."
The fourth one says, "It is a building made of plaster."

When the blind investigators hear each other's reports, they begin to argue.

"Steel?! It is clear the building is made of glass."
"Glass?! You are insane. It's obviously made of wood."
"How could you mistake that building for wood? It is clearly made of plaster."
"Fools! You are all wrong. I am convinced the building is made of steel."

11

In this scenario, the building is the universe – or more specifically and much more relevant to each of us, the building represents the world around us. The building is the Landscape of Being. Except, "the building" has a million different walls made of a million different materials. The blind people in the story are all of humanity – each and every one of us. Each of us approaches "the building," feels it, then reports back what we believe it is made of.

Here's the critical takeaway: Each and every one of us is right. And each and every one of us is wrong.

We are reporting back what we feel using our senses. We reach out with our six senses of vision, hearing, smell, taste, touch and thought, and we report back, "This is what the world is."

And based on what we sense, what we were taught *about* what we sense, and what we think about it *after* we have sensed it; we are right!

The problem with the four blind people and the building was that nobody was able to "see" the building from a big-picture viewpoint. None of the blind people were permitted to walk the perimeter of the entire building, so each one only had the experience of one wall to report on.

Here, in the world around is, we have the same problem. None of us have a big-picture view which encompasses the entire cosmos. All any one of us can see is the small section of reality that we are exposed to. We sense *that* reality and then we make judgements based on that sensory input combined with what we've been taught in the past.

So, when you find out someone who you thought was pretty smart and who you respected went out and voted for someone you thought was not a good candidate for whatever office, you can see how that person might have thought they were seeing things right. From their perspective, they were seeing things right and then making (hopefully) intelligent choices based on this "right seeing." Eight billion people. Eight billion walls.

Using this analogy, we can see that the way to fix the problem of our narrow vision is to pan-out and try to get a big-picture view of the *construct* of reality around us. In our analogy this means we need to "go around the corner" from where we are now and "feel the wall" over on that side. This may give us a different perspective and will likely widen our view and our understanding of the world around us.

If one of the blind people in the four-walled house analogy had walked around the corner, she would have felt a different material there and then had a wider view of reality than her three peers. She would have known that the building was made of at least two different materials while everyone else was convinced the building was made of only one material.

The Cosmology of Not and the Landscape of Being is a way of seeing all of reality as a big-picture which can encompass all other views. Because it is an attempt to get our arms around the entire cosmos, it is all-inclusive and all-accepting.

CHAPTER 1: NOT

To tell this story, we have to start at the beginning. And Not is the beginning. Actually, I will dive into this after we finish the discussion on Not itself, but technically Not is "pre-beginning." Not is the underlying "fabric" on which reality is built. This will make more sense after we finish the deep dive into what Not really is.

In brief, Not is the absolute absence of *everything*. But it turns out that it is not really possible for us to comprehend the absence of everything, so in order to help conceptualize this, I have broken Not down into four distinct attributes. Each of these attributes is a core precept of Not.

The four attributes (core precepts) of Not are coldness, darkness, stasis, and emptiness. Let's dive right in!

COLDNESS

There is no such thing as coldness.

You might respond, "Of course there is! It's cold at the North Pole! It's cold inside the refrigerator! It's cold in deep space!"

Yes, you're right. It can be cold outside, in the refrigerator or in deep space. Allow me to explain what I mean.

What I mean by saying there is no such thing as coldness, is that by itself, coldness does not exist as a thing which can be manipulated, carried, added to or removed from a system.

We cannot take a bit of coldness and add it to a system to make that system colder.

For me, the first counter argument that comes to mind is ice. Isn't ice a bit of coldness that we add to a system (a drink) to make the system colder?

Practically speaking, that's certainly true. But *actually*, what is happening is that the ice is not *adding* cold to the liquid, but rather it is drawing heat *out* of the liquid (and into itself). And as a result of taking on this heat, the ice begins to melt and the liquid around the ice becomes colder.

I'm talking about thermodynamics and heat transfer. The way heat transfer works is that warmth will always move to that which is colder than itself. This is why air that is warm moves to the areas of the air which are colder – thus the reason we have breezes and wind.

You might ask, "So what? What difference does it make if it's the warmth moving to the cold or the cold moving to the warmth?"

In our everyday lives, it usually doesn't matter. But the difference is real, and it is significant.

The significance of this is that the *warmth* is what we can control. The *warmth* is what we can contain, carry, add, and remove from the system.

If we add warmth to a system, the system becomes warmer. If we remove warmth from a system, the system becomes colder. Either way, it is warmth that we are adding and removing, not coldness.

There are two more common counter arguments I would like to address: a refrigerator and space.

In the case of a refrigerator, you might argue that it is cold inside the refrigerator and that when you place food inside, the refrigerator moves coldness into the food. But this is not the case. True to the laws of thermodynamics, the refrigerator is not producing cold and adding it to the food. Instead, the refrigerator is removing warmth from inside. Thus, when you place some food in the refrigerator, the refrigerator begins to remove the warmth from the food and that warmth is sent outside the refrigerator. Put your hand near the back and you will feel the warmth pouring out. (The same is true if you place your hand over an air conditioner condenser fan outside a building on a hot summer day. You will feel the warmth that the air conditioner is removing from the building). You see? Warmth is what the refrigerator is manipulating in order to arrive at a certain level of coldness.

What about space? Isn't the temperature of space called "absolute zero?" This is the coldest temperature there is, right? I used to think that. But space has a couple of surprises. Absolute zero *is* the coldest temperature but space is ever so slightly warmer than that. Apparently, space, even in the most "empty" and remote parts of it, has some quantum activity. Stranger, perhaps, and easy to forget even after you've learned it once or twice, is that space is not a 'lack of stuff' but rather an actual substance. Space is made of something. Space is some kind of material that is actually expanding. What it is made of is still up for debate. Part of it, though, among other things, is evidently dark matter and/or dark energy. So, yes, space is about as cold as it gets, but no, space is not perfect coldness devoid of all warmth.

Remember I started this discussion on coldness by claiming that coldness, as a thing that might exist independently of other things, does not exist. Over the last few paragraphs, I have argued that coldness does not exist. But I have also argued that if we could remove all warmth, we would have nothing left *but* coldness. Thus, my argument is really twofold: One, that coldness does not exist, and two, that coldness must exist. Paradox is prevalent in truth. As something which cannot exist and therefore must exist, coldness is one of the four core precepts of Not.

Coldness does not exist, but because warmth exists, coldness must exist. One might make the argument that this is simply the nature of naming things. For instance, in order for there to be a front, there must be a back or in order for there to be an outside, there must also be an inside. In other words, that warmth versus coldness is merely a matter of semantics. But that is not the case. You can achieve varying levels of coldness by altering the warmth, but no amount of altering the "front" of something will make the "back" be less "back" than it already is. Front and back are very black and white definitions. Conceptually, coldness and warmth are not dualities like front and back or inside and outside.

Having these two attributes (1. a mandate to exist and 2. being a core precept of Not), coldness is a base attribute of existence that is "always there." And on top of this base precept, warmth can be added or subtracted. But underneath the warmth will always be this perfect and pure coldness that cannot be moved, altered, or affected in any way. Absolute coldness is pure, perfect, and exists independently of warmth.

Underneath all warmth, will always be this base precept, "coldness." And the only way to experience it would be to remove all the warmth. Removing all warmth, however, is not possible. As such, we can never achieve perfect coldness. We can never arrive at this core, pure and perfect base precept.

But let's, just for the sake of argument, say that such a perfect and pure coldness *could* exist. If it really could exist, we could never know about it.

This is because of the Observer Effect. The fact that just by virtue of observation, the observer alters the thing which is being observed. Measuring the air pressure in a tire is a good example of this. Let's say you have a tire with a pressure of

33.6 PSI. When you press the tire gauge onto the valve, there is a slight hiss as some air leaks out. Now the pressure is 33.5 PSI (and that's the number that now shows up on the gauge). Removing the gauge might produce another slight hiss and now that you have finished measuring the tire, the tire pressure is 33.4 PSI, even though the gauge-reading is still at 33.5 PSI. You see, just by observing the tire pressure (which was 33.6) you have altered the original tire pressure from 33.6 PSI to 33.4 PSI. You caused the tire pressure to change twice and ironically your tire gauge reading of 33.5 PSI does not capture either one of the changes you caused by measuring the pressure to begin with, nor does it reflect the actual tire pressure once you finished taking your measurement. By "observing" the pressure, you have changed it.

The same is true with coldness. By attempting to measure perfect coldness, your measuring device would necessarily introduce some warmth, thereby "ruining" the perfection of the coldness you were trying to measure (E.g. the coldness would be a little warmer than it was before you tried to measure it).

By acknowledging the Observer Effect, we have established that if perfect coldness *could* exist, we could not know about it (because by "knowing" about it, we make it not perfect anymore). We cannot know about or *experience* perfect coldness. And if there exists something we can never know about or experience, then it may as well not exist at all.

So, we can infer the existence of coldness by talking about heat transfer, but coldness, by itself cannot exist.

It is this paradoxically overlapping "extantness" and inability to exist that give coldness the quality of being an attribute of Not.

Let's move on to the second precept of Not, darkness.

DARKNESS

There is no such thing as darkness.

"What?" you respond, "Of course there is! It is dark when you turn off the lights. It is dark at night. Speaking of refrigerators, it is dark inside the refrigerator when the door is closed."

True, it is darker in those places, but just like coldness being a state you can only achieve by the removal of warmth, darkness is a state you can only arrive at by removing light. In any given system, if you remove some light from that system, that system will become darker. As more and more light is removed, the system becomes darker and darker.

If you remove *all* light from a system, you will be left with *pure* darkness. The ultimate in darkness. Perfect darkness. Perfection is subjective, but I can still safely say that this darkness I describe would be perfect because there could be nothing darker. There could be no darkness that is darker. In being dark, this darkness – where *all* light has been removed – would be the ultimate achievement in darkness. Thus, it would be perfect darkness. And something that is perfect is, well, *perfect*.

Like coldness, you cannot carry darkness around with you and insert it into a system where there is light thereby making that system darker. The only way to make a system darker is by reducing the amount of light in that system. By removing light, you make a room darker. Adding light, makes the room lighter (less dark). We cannot make a room darker by "adding darkness."

It is as if darkness is the canvas on which the room is painted with light. Darkness is the underlying infrastructure "on which" light may exist.

Nowhere in all of existence is there such thing as this perfect darkness I describe. The reason it cannot exist is because there is always, somewhere, a stream or wave of photons (particles of light). Even if it is just a single photon, or a subatomic particle, there is technically energy (a form of light) there.

Imagine, for a moment, you are floating in space somewhere. Can you see stars in the distance? Even stars that might be billions of light years away? If you can see a star – any star – that means there is a stream of photons flooding into your eyes from that star. It means that the space between you and that star has light streaming through it (or at least it did at some point in time). Needless to say, if light is streaming through that space, that space is not "dark."

Nonetheless, let's imagine for a moment that we have created a perfect darkness and now we want to observe it.

If one were to construct a device within which there were no photons, then theoretically one would have created the perfect darkness I describe. But it still could not be detected by the human eye. It could only be known to us through some readout from some device created to detect it. I would posit that where there is molecular activity one will find a photon or quantum influx of energy which can be interpreted as light. Therefore, the detecting of perfect darkness in and of itself would "infect" that darkness with one or more particles of light thereby making it no longer a pure and perfect darkness.

Paradoxically, darkness *must* exist for there to be light, even though darkness without light cannot exist. This is a fundamental aspect of darkness that is difficult to describe. Darkness is to light as a canvas is to a painting. Darkness will always be there, deep beneath the surface of light, waiting to be revealed. In this way, a perfect darkness *must* exist.

Like coldness, darkness is not something we can manipulate directly. Only through light can we understand darkness. And a perfect darkness *cannot* exist. Again, we have a paradox.

Thus, darkness is the second of the four core precepts that make up Not.

STASIS

There is no such thing as stasis.

What is that supposed to mean?

First, what I mean by 'stasis' is a measure of activity. Or, rather, in this case, a measure of inactivity. An active system is not a static system. A system with no activity would be a static system. An absolutely static system would be a system in perfect stasis. Imagine an empty room that has a layer of dust in it. There are no objects in the room and there is no movement in the room. It is completely still. Or is it?

It may appear that way on the surface but this room is not really in stasis. Inside each speck of dust is a cosmic explosion of molecular activity. Within the trillions of molecules in each single dust speck are countless trillions of atoms binding, spinning, attracting and repelling each other. Within the atoms are quintillions more subatomic particles in a quantum dance with each other zinging and whizzing around and these particles have bindings and associations with other particles possibly trillions of light years away in quantum entanglements and other quantum sub-arrangements we have yet to comprehend.

In short, like coldness and darkness, stasis is a concept but not a "thing." In other words, we cannot walk up to an active system and add some "stasis" to make the system less active. We can *remove* activity from a system to arrive at a static system, but we cannot add stillness, stasis, or "inactivity" to a system to make it less active.

Complete and utter stasis is something that cannot be achieved in actual existence. But, like coldness and darkness, if it could be achieved, a state of absolute stasis would represent a form of absolute perfection. Absolute stasis could not be more static and would therefore be *perfectly* static. Thus, in that regard, absolute stasis would be perfection.

Why can we not achieve perfect stasis? A system that is perfectly static would be a system with no molecular activity whatsoever. It would be a system with no atomic activity. A system with no subatomic activity. The reason we cannot achieve this is because ultimately everything is comprised of energy and energy cannot stop being "energetic."

A group of atoms or molecules that have no subatomic activity whatsoever is a theoretical concept at best. It is a state of existence we cannot create or measure. Just like coldness and darkness, an attempt to measure a completely static system would introduce an *active* measuring device, thereby causing activity to enter the system. The theoretical state of 'perfect stasis' would be "infected" with activity and no longer be purely static.

Similar to what we see with coldness and darkness, underlying all activity is "a promise" of stasis, though that promise may never be fulfilled. *Can* never be fulfilled. Stasis is a fundamental base over which activity exists, but activity cannot cease in order to reveal this underlying stasis. Paradoxically, stasis must exist as an underlying stratum to existence itself but cannot exist independently of activity.

Thus, stasis is the third of the four core precepts that make up Not.

This brings us to emptiness.

EMPTINESS

There is no such thing as emptiness. That sounds a little bit mystic, a little bit cosmic and a lot bit metaphysical. But if you have followed along from the previous discussions on the four core precepts that make up Not, you will see immediately how this must be the case.

There cannot be a pure state of emptiness because there must always be something present to discern the emptiness. (If no presence is there to discern the emptiness, how can one know that there was emptiness there to begin with)? And as soon as some presence is there to witness the emptiness, the system is no longer empty.

For this discussion we consider a "presence" to be some conglomeration of atoms. A rock, a tree, a flower, a sun or a person are all things considered to be a "presence." But even smaller groupings of atoms are a presence. Any warmth, light or activity must necessarily also be "a presence." You see, in any given system one considers "empty," if nothing else, there must exist the *presence* of warmth, light or activity. Thus, no system can truly be empty.

Space is not empty. In fact, in our discussion on coldness, we already covered the point that space is actually a substance. But going back momentarily to the example we considered in the discussion on darkness, imagine you are floating in space somewhere. Can you see stars in the distance? If you can see a star – any star – (as previously mentioned) then that means, there is a stream of photons flooding into your eyes from that star. This means that the space between you and that star has light streaming through it. It is not *empty* space. It is not emptiness.

Like coldness, darkness and stasis, one cannot take emptiness and deliver it to some system of presence(s) to reduce the amount of presence. To arrive at emptiness, you can only remove presence. You cannot add emptiness.

If you could remove all presence from a system you could then achieve a state of absolute and perfect emptiness. The perfection of the emptiness is implicit because a system that contains absolutely no presence would be the ultimate in emptiness. It could not become emptier. If it cannot become emptier, then it is perfectly empty. If nothing else can be removed, it is the pinnacle of emptiness. In this way, the emptiness I describe represents a certain purity. Perfection.

Again, we have the paradox of *mandatory actuality* (emptiness must exist when all presence is removed) overlaid with the inability for the attribute to exist (emptiness cannot exist because there must be a presence there to "know" the emptiness exists). It is as if emptiness exists as a fundamental underlying basis for presence to fill. We can imagine emptiness because we know there are places that exist when we are not in those places. But even when we (as presence) are not in those places, there is still warmth, light, activity and the presence of energy and quanta in those places and for this reason, no place may be truly empty.

Emptiness is the last of the four core precepts that make up Not.

PERFECT TRUTHS

Coldness, darkness, stasis, and emptiness are the four core precepts of Not. As such, Not is simply defined as "cold, dark, static emptiness."

In describing the four core precepts of Not, we have established that none of them are attributes that truly exist. Or, again, if they can exist it doesn't matter to us, because we can never know about their existence.

Thus, the same is true with Not. Not cannot exist. Or, if it can exist, we can never know about it. The experiencing of Not would change Not into not being Not anymore by the entity which was doing the experiencing.

Not is "the canvas" on which All is painted using the paints of warmth, light, activity, and presence. However, there is a caveat: the paint can never *experience* the canvas.

Underneath all of life, underneath everything that was, is, or can be, there is always this basis of Not, "waiting" to be "revealed." In this way, Not is the ultimate in occulted knowledge.

This is why I said earlier that Not is actually "pre-beginning." Not is beneath the substrate of reality. Not is the backdrop *behind* reality. Conceptually, Not is the "infrastructure" on which reality exists. It is the stratum underlying the cosmos – the ground which exists underneath the foundation on which reality is built.

If you paint a picture of the cosmos and place Not at the bottom, as the basis on which all of reality rests, then there would be nothing depicted underneath Not. Nothing can exist beyond Not. Again, if it did, it would touch Not, thereby changing Not into something that isn't Not.

Not is the absolute absence of everything. The word "absolute" automatically implies perfection. Once we have removed everything, there is nothing left to remove. In this way, Not is perfect. In this complete lack of anything else, Not is absolute purity and perfection. (Not cannot be any Nottier than it already is. It is the Nottest!)

Not is also certainty. Not is the certainty of "nothing else." In this certainty, we find an ultimate truth. Facts may be disputed. "That which is known," can change as new knowledge is gained and new facts are discovered. But "truth" cannot change. Truth is absolute. Like Not, truth is also the purity of perfection. Hence, Not is perfection and Not is true.

Not is an incredibly powerful concept because through understanding Not we immediately see that everything *must* exist. I'm going to say that again and give it its own paragraph because it seems so absurdly obvious that it may be easily taken for granted.

Everything *must* exist.

When I say everything, I mean *everything!* All of it.

In fact, in the Cosmology of Not, I refer to *everything* by just using the word, "All."

Chapter 1.5: Jump Point, Not to All

Somehow from nothing we jump to everything. Most religions call this "creation." Our science has not yet dropped beneath the "All-horizon," so we do not know how it is possible to go from nothing to something.

But just because science cannot yet explain it doesn't mean the religions have it right. "Creation" has its own problems... For instance, if there was truly nothing, then there could not have been a creator. So, where did the creator come from? A Big Bang? If a Big Bang *made* a creator, then couldn't a Big Bang have made a universe too? Why *make* a creator at all?

It turns out this jump from nothing to something is a jump that all cosmologies have to make.

The science of Cosmology has many theories which might explain how the universe came to exist. By far, the most well-known theory is the Big Bang Theory, so in the Cosmology of Not, we will also use the Big Bang Theory as our "assumption" for how the universe came into existence.

Simply stated, the Big Bang Theory postulates that the universe exploded into existence from an infinitely small point, referred to as a "quantum singularity." There was a quantum singularity. It exploded. The universe is that explosion and it's still expanding outward from that initial detonation.

I would like to talk a little more about the quantum singularity and the Big Bang, but first we need to touch on the Scattering of All.

CHAPTER 2: ALL

We defined Not as cold, dark, static emptiness, so to arrive at Not:

We had to remove *all* warmth to arrive at perfect coldness.

We had to remove *all* light to arrive at perfect darkness.

We had to remove *all* activity to arrive at perfect stasis.

We had to remove *all* presence to arrive at perfect emptiness.

The fact that warmth, light, activity, and presence existed to begin with (in order for us to remove them), we take as a proof for the existence of warmth, light, activity, and presence. In other words, warmth is an axiom for warmth because there is no fundamental proof for the existence of warmth other than the fact that warmth exists.

The same is true for light, activity, and presence. "Light exists," is an axiom for the existence of light. Light just is. We know light exists because we see that light exists. As a footnote, it turns out that the perfect darkness of Not *also* proves that light exists.

"Activity exists," is an axiom for activity; activity exists *because* there is activity. And you probably won't be surprised that the perfect stasis of Not acts as a secondary proof for the existence activity.

And finally, presence is an axiom for presence. That there is something present is proven true in that there is something present proving presence is real. It is almost absurd to belabor this point, but it is worth drilling down *this* deeply into the definitions of warmth, light, activity, and presence because these four attributes are the constituent "components" of All. They are the fundamental building blocks of reality.

Warmth, light, activity, and presence, when taken together, are everything that Not isn't. In fact, everything that isn't Not, *is everything*.

In other words, if it isn't Not, it is All else. Or stated in yet another way: that which is not cold, dark, static, emptiness is instead, warm, light, active, presence.

That which isn't Not is All.

In the chapter on Not, we said that Not is the absolute absence of *everything*. Hence, All is the absolute presence of *everything*.

How did Not come to be? Or is asking how Not came to be an absurd question in that Not just *is*? Perhaps it is not an absurd question because, while we know that Not just is, we also know that Not cannot exist.

While Not can both exist and not exist simultaneously, All is different. All exists, and must exist, and (in all likelihood) cannot not exist (in other words, warm light active presence cannot go away). As a sidenote, there's a neat side effect to this mandate. The fact that warm, light, active, presence cannot stop existing means that we – as warm, light, active, presence – will always *be* in one form or another. Did I just say "form?" Sorry, I'm getting ahead of myself. We'll talk about Form in Chapter 3.

How did warm light active presence come into existence? Especially if Not existed prior to All? In other words, how could there have been pure and perfect nothingness and then the Scattering of All?

I don't know how All came to be. I don't know why it came to be. All I know is that Not defines it. Not clarifies All. Not establishes All's absolute existence and its truth. And All is fundamental in that it is just four attributes (warmth, light, activity, and presence). Each of these attributes can quasi-embody other objects, so when warmth, light, activity, and presence are combined they become all-inclusive to a god, a Big Bang, a sun, a universe, a multiverse, etc. In other words, those things must be construed from warmth, light, activity, and presence, just as All is. All is "the Scattering" of warm, light, active presence underneath everything that exists.

Not and All. There is a significant difference between these two dualities. Not *must* exist but *cannot* exist. So, with Not there is confusion surrounding this perfect paradox.

But with All, there is no confusion. All *must* exist, period. There can be no doubt as to the existence of All. If I haven't been clear about this yet, the reason All must exist is because we have already established that Not cannot exist, so if we were to remove All, we would be left with "that which cannot be" (Not). Thus, All *must* exist. And in this way, it turns out that All is another perfect truth.

Not is the underlying "strata" for reality, because Not defines reality – perhaps somehow *causes* reality? I started Chapter 1 by saying that Not defines reality. Not defines All.

And, All *is* reality. All is everything.

THE SCATTERING

Now that we have introduced the idea of "everything," and we have defined everything as being constructed from the four fundamental building blocks of warmth, light, activity, and presence, we should come up with a model of how everything got here.

Luckily, science has already given us a beautiful description of how this might have happened.

The warm, light, active presence of All is also referred to as the Scattering. All is the chaotic Scattering of warmth, light, activity, and presence. In the Metaphysics of Not, it is quite clear that no matter how deeply we zoom into the building blocks of reality, we will always find warmth, light, activity, and presence. We find these attributes in a cell, a molecule, an atom, a subatomic particle, an elementary (or "fundamental") particle, and we find them in the superstring. And I believe, when we get there, we must find these same attributes of warmth, light, activity, and presence beneath the superstring. When science breaks down the superstring into component pieces, whatever we end up calling those pieces, they will be comprised of warmth, light, activity, and presence.

Let's take a moment for a quick thought experiment. Imagine the Big Bang. In layman's terms, the Big Bang is described as a quantum singularity which instantaneously detonated in an incomprehensible explosion of raw energy. To summarize a billion years in a single sentence, the pure energy that exploded outward "cooled" into quantities of various gases such as hydrogen and helium and over time these swirling clouds of gases coalesced into stars, planets, and galaxies. Perhaps before the quantum singularity exploded, it could be described as "order," but whatever the case, the explosion of energy that resulted from the Big Bang we can certainly describe as pure chaos.

The Metaphysics of Not posits that in the Big Bang theory, the fundamental building blocks of that quantum singularity were warmth, light, activity, and presence. And therefore, the underlying attributes of everything which exploded outward from the singularity were also warmth, light, activity, and presence.

It might be tempting to imagine that the quantum singularity was sitting all by itself in the middle of Not. However, since the quantum singularity was warm, light, active presence, it could not possibly have been touching the cold, dark, static emptiness of Not. Logically, Not and All can never touch. For, if they did touch, the instant the singularity made contact with Not, Not would no longer be Not.

So, what was surrounding the singularity? What did the Big Bang explode *into*? And subsequently what is our universe expanding into this very moment? While we (apparently) cannot know that yet, what we can be certain of is that the universe is not expanding into Not. If it were, then it would render Not into something other than perfect cold, dark, static emptiness. It would render Not into no longer being Not.

So, while there is much we don't yet know, there are some things we have established so far:
1.   Not must exist; Not cannot exist.
2.   All does exist and must always exist.
3.   The Scattering of All did not come from Not.
4.   The Scattering of All does not exist within Not.

The Scattering, then, is the great expanse of warm, light, active presence that constructs all of existence. One way to imagine this is to imagine a ball-pit you might find at funhouse for kids.

THE BALL PIT

In the Alchemy of Not, we assign colors to the attributes of warmth, light, activity, and presence in order to use them or refer to them visually.
Warmth: Orange
Light: Yellow
Activity: Red
Presence: Green

Imagine, then, a ball pit where each of the balls are one of those four colors. The only thing in the pit are orange, yellow, red and green balls. But this pit is huge. It has trillions and trillions of balls. The pit is filled with warmth, light, activity, and presence. This is chaos. This is warmth, light, activity, and presence with no form.

Now expand the ball pit to encompass all of time and space and shrink the warmth, light, activity, and presence-balls down to nearly infinitely small points. This Scattering of warmth, light, activity, and presence points are the everything and everywhere of chaos.

UNITY

We have established that warmth, light, activity, and presence are the fundamental building blocks of everything in existence. This bears mentioning again because I need to address one more reference we can make to All. It is the Unity of All.

This is a sneak-peak into the next chapter because for the Unity of All to make more sense, we need to have Form. And for the Unity of All to have spiritual significance to us, we need to sneak a peek into Chapter 5 on the Spirit-Consciousness.

But for now, I would like to just draw your attention to the point that everything is made of warm, light, active presence. This means planets, stars, desks, trees, apples, sticks, dogs, cats and certainly people.

We are all inter-connected in many ways, but if in no other way, none can deny that we are all built of the same fundamental particles that everything else is built of. When we break down any one of us into the smallest constituent flickers, it will be the four attributes of warmth, light, activity and presence. You are warm, light, active presence and I am warm, light, active presence. We are both made of the same stuff. We are both warm, light, active presence. And in this, there is perfect Unity in All.

CHAPTER 2.5: JUMP POINT, ALL TO FORM

Somehow, warmth, light, activity, and presence must have begun to coalesce into pairs, triads, quads, etc., until distinctions in the chaos began to appear.

"Distinctions of chaos" would necessarily be "pockets of order." From chaos came order. (Of course, the original quantum singularity might be described as a perfectly ordered set of warmth, light, activity, and presence, in which case we could also point out that chaos came from order before order came from chaos.)

Continuing our ascent from Not, and All, when order appeared in chaos, we then had Form.

CHAPTER 3: FORM (IS)

We began with Not and from there we derived All. While this almost seems like circular logic (defining Not by removing All and then claiming that All had to exist in order to define Not), it is nonetheless airtight logic. After all, who can dispute the existence of warmth, light, activity, and presence?

We can refer to All as a scattering of warmth, light, activity, and presence. In a very real sense, the Scattering is pure chaos.

From a cosmological perspective, we can look back at the origin of reality and imagine that (perhaps) there was Not. And "on top" of Not, across a "chasm of actuality," we can imagine the Scattering of warmth, light, activity, and presence.

As we climb this cosmological ladder explaining existence, the next rung has to be Form. Somehow, from the chaotic scattering of warmth, light, activity, and presence, there came to be an ordering of Form. Form is the structured conglomeration of warmth, light, activity, and presence.

What did the first forms look like? Were they superstrings of vibrating warm, light, active presence? Were they more fundamental than even the superstring?

We don't know what the first forms looked like, but we do know that layers upon layers of Form constructed new forms and that ultimately, we achieved forms such as the hydrogen and the helium atoms.

Even more complex forms must have followed this same path, so that there then existed lithium, carbon, oxygen, etc.

From here we speculate that conglomerations of these "atom forms" came together to create even larger and more complex forms such as molecules, cells, and other materials we call "matter."

And matter, mixed and matched with energies of various sorts, formed suns and planets.

And suns and planets were pulled together into large groupings called solar systems and these solar systems, in turn, gathered together into massive organizations called galaxies.

When we group enough galaxies together, we can call them galactic clusters. These clusters of galaxies, when grouped together, form galactic superclusters.

And as of this writing, we speculate that the universe itself is a conglomeration of galactic superclusters. Are there other universes which group together to form a multiverse? Do multiverses group together in massive arrays we might call an omniverse? And omniverses group together to form pan-omniverses?

And so on and so on…

While there are countless mysteries here (beginning with Not, moving into how All became, then the mystery of Form itself), there is also a logical progression here that begins to tell a story. The story being told is the Cosmology of Not.

CHAPTER 3.5: JUMP POINT, FORM TO AWARENESS

Somehow, from inanimate Forms, we jump to animated Forms. This is the leap from lifelessness to life itself! Here, again, religion might simply say, "Creation!"

And again, the question of "What *did* the creating?" would have to be asked. If there is a *something* which "created" life (E.g., a god, perhaps?) then how did that god *become* to begin with? There was chaos and then there was a god? Again, why the middleman? As you can see, each one of these Jump Points is an unsolved mystery in human evolution and universal cosmological history.

This is still a mystery as our science has not yet explained how lifeless energy and chemical matter somehow became aware of its surroundings and swirled into becoming "life."

But just because there is an unsolved mysterious jump point doesn't mean it didn't happen. We know it happened because there is life.

CHAPTER 4: AWARENESS (IT IS)

We began this cosmology with nothing (the cold, dark, static, emptiness of Not), then jumped to everything (the warm, light, active, presence of All), and then we acknowledged "stuff" that formed within the Scattering of All: Form. Hence, we have atoms, molecules, stars, and planets. In the stars, we can imagine infernos of pure raw energy blasting subatomic particles and atoms into the substance we call space. And around these stars we can imagine gaseous and solid planets. And on these planets, we can imagine alien and unseen gases, liquids and metals forming skyscapes, seascapes, and landscapes.

What we've described up to now is Not, All and Form.

It is time to introduce another mystery as we take the next leap. The next rung in the ladder of our ascent from Not is Awareness.

The leap we had to take to get from Form to Awareness is a huge leap. It spans both life and sentience. Awareness is a side effect of living and so in order to talk about Awareness we need to talk about life.

What happened between Chapter 3 and Chapter 4 that life all of a sudden came to exist?

How did gases, liquids and metals suddenly become living matter?

Fascinatingly, nobody knows the answer to those questions. With all of our progress in the various sciences, we still don't know how the universe went from not having life to having life. The child's version of the story here on Earth is that there was a primordial ooze and then "lightning struck" and the first living cells were born. This story of the origin of life is just as far reaching and desperate as "the Big Bang" theory of how the universe came into being or the idea that a big man in the sky just "made it happen."

In each chapter of the Cosmology of Not, we must make these same fantastic leaps that our modern science has had to make in order for us to keep on moving upward. If we don't take such leaps, we could never get anywhere.

As I've already mentioned, truly, we don't know how Form came to be either. We speculate that there was a Big Bang and that gasses coalesced into the forms described in Chapter 3, but this is speculation based on our current limited mathematics and theoretical hypotheses. We don't know how Form came to be. But who can deny that there are Forms?

The same is true with life. We don't know how life came to be, but who can deny that life exists? (Perhaps ironically, only life can deny the existence of life – but we'll get more into that aspect of life in Chapter 5).

With life comes sentience – the ability to sense one's surroundings. When these senses group together, another trait of life forms within the lifeform: Awareness.

Awareness is essentially a knowledge about one's surroundings. This can be defined simply as the knowledge of warmth, light, activity, and presence. A lifeform might sense heat and move away from it (or toward it). Plants, for instance, sense light and turn their leaves toward the light in order to feed on it.

Does non-life have sentience or Awareness? From our perspective, as living things, it is easy to make the claim that non-living things do not have sentience or Awareness. In fact, all we have to do to ensure that only life has Awareness is to define Awareness as something which only life can possess. In this way, the game is certainly rigged against the inanimate.

But whether or not the inanimate has Awareness, we can certainly feel confident in making the claim that life has Awareness. As life, ourselves, we know this to be true.

Life having Awareness, allowed life to move around, up and down and to-and-fro. We can now break down Forms into two groups: that which is aware (alive, animated) and that which is unaware (not alive, inanimate).

But it is important to point out here, that even though we are breaking Form into two different groups, all Forms are still comprised of the same essential building blocks of warmth, light, activity, and presence.

There are clumps of warm, light, active presence which are not aware and there are clumps of warm, light, active presence which are aware.

CHAPTER 4.5: JUMP POINT, AWARENESS TO SPIRIT-CONSCIOUSNESS

As we ascend from Not and All, we climb through Form and Awareness but then another critical distinction occurs. Somehow, Awareness becomes aware of the fact that it exists. Awareness becomes aware of itself. Thus, a new aspect of life is introduced: self-awareness.

How did this happen? How is it that some sentient lifeform moving about from here to there and from hither to thither suddenly became aware of the fact that it was aware of its surroundings? How did life suddenly garner the ability to reflect on its own thoughts? How did consciousness form? When did consciousness form? Did it begin as something else (like the Bicameral Mind[5]) and then evolve? Is it evolving still? Will artificial intelligence achieve this rung in the ascent through the Progression of Awakening? Do "lesser lifeforms" have consciousness? Do inanimate objects have consciousness?[6]

All of these questions remain unsolved mysteries which we must just accept as we leap from one stage of the evolution of the Self to the next.

CHAPTER 5: SPIRIT-CONSCIOUSNESS (I AM)

The next rung on the cosmological ladder and the next leap we must take – as this too remains a complete mystery to both religion and science – is what religion calls the soul (or spirit) and what science calls consciousness. For all intents and

---

[5] Julian Jaynes, The Origin of Consciousness in the Breakdown of the Bicameral Mind
[6] See Panpsychism.

purposes, this is also where we, as reflections of the universe, begin. The Spirit-Consciousness is the genesis of the Self.

Nobody knows what a soul is, and nobody knows what consciousness is. In fact, it turns out that it is extremely difficult to even define either term.

In the interest of simplicity and for the sake of conversation, I would like to define consciousness simply as "our awareness or our own awareness." And I believe that this awareness of our own awareness is also what most people think of when they think of the terms, "soul" or "spirit."

There are many people who believe that human beings (and perhaps some or all other animals) have a soul. The soul, in the way I am talking about it, is synonymous with the spirit.

There are others who do not believe in the spirit (aka. soul) but acknowledge that human beings (and perhaps some or all other animals) have a consciousness.

In order to address both schools of thought, I merge these terms into the all-inclusive, "Spirit-Consciousness." Think of the Spirit-Consciousness as the one who is reading these words to your mind. Or perhaps it is the one your mind is reading these words to? It is the inner being with which your mind regularly dialogues. Where pertinent, the Spirit-Consciousness is also what embodies your "inner child." When we talk about "spirituality," we're talking about addressing the Spirit-Consciousness. Those who believe in the divine would call the Spirit-Consciousness, "the divinity within."

The Spirit-Consciousness is the next tier in the Cosmology of Not as it takes the Awareness of life from Chapter 4 and escalates it into the awareness of its own Awareness.

It is here, in Chapter 5, that we first become aware of our own existence. Hence, for most of us (me included), the Spirit-Consciousness becomes the first tier in the cosmology of the Self.[7] Recall that the life from Chapter 4 was aware of its surroundings but it was not aware of itself. Here, with the introduction of the Spirit-Consciousness, life becomes self-aware.

The Spirit-Consciousness is the progenitor of the Self. In the Self as a reflection of the universe, The Spirit-Consciousness is the Big Bang of the Self, but it is also the quantum singularity that becomes the Big Bang. So, it is the seed of new order which will flow into chaos, and it is the source of the chaos that results from the explosion of *being*. E.g., we begin as Order, and we become Chaos which in turn seeks to re-order itself later in life.

Remember, we took a leap to get here. We do not know how life *became*, we do not know how life became *aware* and we do not know how that which was aware became *aware of its own awareness*. These are all fantastic unsolved mysteries!

Regardless of whether you come from the spirit side of the house or the consciousness side of the house, the Spirit-

---

[7] It is possible that through a regular, deep meditation practice, one might drop below this level, down to the Awareness level, or possibly even deeper, down to Form. I have yet to try this, personally. If Nirvana is real, it seems it would likely be found even deeper than this, all the way down in the Scattering of All.

Consciousness is very real. But, if you should have any doubts, there is a way for you to realize this truth on your own.

Humans have been proving their own existence to themselves since before we could write. There is evidence of this in the ancient writings of the Vedas and we know that these things that were written are thousands of years old and were copied from oral traditions that stretch back into the darkness of pre-written history.

For modernity – and especially those of us in the Western world, a more concrete and understandable example of this "proof of consciousness" is captured in a meditation described by Renes Descartes in his work titled *Meditations on First Philosophy*, published in 1641 CE.

In this thought experiment, Descartes asks us to imagine away our senses. We are to think away our vision, hearing, taste, smell, and touch. Once we have imagined away our senses, we are left with only our thoughts. Descartes then asks us to imagine that our thoughts may not really be ours. He suggests that they could have been fabricated *for us* to make us *think* they are ours – like a dream or a computer simulation.

If our thoughts are not really our thoughts, then they cannot be trusted, so he suggests we should also imagine our thoughts away. Think away your thoughts. If you are following along, then you should now be at a stage where you have thought away all of your senses (leaving you "sitting there" with only thought) and now you've also thought away your thinking. Once you are only thought, and you think away your thought, what is left?

If you have not already done this, I recommend you try it sometime. It is a reality-checking, grounding, and mind-blowing experience. Once you drop down *that* deeply into your own thought – to the level where using thought itself, you have thought away everything including thought – you come to this crystal clear and strikingly simple realization that you truly and absolutely exist. Or at least that *something* which is thinking does.[8] When Descartes reached this realization he said the famous words, "cogito ergo sum" ("I think, therefore I am.")

I have tried this thought experiment myself and I have yet to experience a clearer proof of the existence of my own Spirit-Consciousness. I think of this as my Self.

So, it is here in Chapter 5 that we establish our first proof of the Self. This seed of Spirit-Consciousness later sprouts into the tree of Self that each of us grows into as we continue to rise up: from the depths of Not, to the Shallows of the Ocean of Consciousness.

Beginning here, the story of Not becomes the story of Self. The Cosmology of Not begins to overlap with the Cosmology of the Self.

Now that we exist as something distinct from the stars, landscapes, animals, and other variations of Form and Awareness, we realize that our own cosmology – the Cosmology of the Self – is the same story that is told by any and all other cosmologies. It now becomes clear that the Cosmology of Not tells the story of the beginning, progression, and end of Self as a perfect reflection of the beginning, progression, and end of the Universe, of which each Self is a unique reflection.

---

[8] I call this the Self. If you don't believe in a Self, then this would be the "no Self" equivalent.

The Spirit-Consciousness is the Big-Bang of the Self. It is the genesis of what we later become, and it is the great fire that shines forth as the animation of *being*. It is our innermost core of the pure energy of thought.

The Spirit-Consciousness is, "I am." It is proof of its own existence. Just as science is not yet able to know for sure what was happening before the Big Bang of the universe, we as individual Selves, are unable to know for sure what was going on before the Big Bang of the Self.[9] Going only on what we know, we have to assume that the Spirit-Consciousness is no more responsible for being an aspect of Self than Awareness was responsible for being an aspect of life. In other words, the Spirit-Consciousness is not to be rewarded or penalized for existing. The Spirit-Consciousness does not need permission to burn brightly in the black of existence any more than a sun needs permission to shine in space. The Spirit-Consciousness does not need permission to exist. It does not need authorization to *be*. It just *is*. This has another implication: The Spirit-Consciousness cannot experience guilt. The Spirit-Consciousness knows it is okay for it to *be* because it *is*.

Like the axioms of each of the previous chapters, the Spirit-Consciousness is an axiom for the existence of the Spirit-Consciousness. We have a right to *be* here because we *are* here.

CHAPTER 5.5: JUMP POINT, SPIRIT-CONSCIOUSNESS TO AUTHORIZATION

When the Self is born, it is essentially "a baby in the basket." It is a newly formed (or newly "born"?) consciousness which

---

[9] Scientifically speaking. That is to say, notwithstanding knowledge gained from past life regressions, pre-existence, reincarnation, and the like.

is staring wide-eyed at the chaos of the world around it asking, "Who am I? What am I? Where, when, why, and how am I?"

While each one of those six very specific questions carry a tremendous amount of punch to them, there is one commonality in the various answers. The commonality in the answers to the who, what, where, when, why, and how of the Self lies in Authorization for being.

While it seems that Authorization for being is initially sought externally, when we drop this deeply into the Self, we realize that Authorization for being actually came *from* the Spirit-Consciousness. We ended Chapter 5 with the understanding that we have a right to be here because we are here.

That very idea is the only Authorization we need to be who and what we are. Who am I? I. What am I? I am.

Thou art that.

I am authorized to *be* here because I *am* here.

CHAPTER 6: AUTHORIZATION (TO BE)

One of the mysteries science has yet to unravel is the mystery of entropy. Entropy is a thermodynamic concept that measures the amount of randomness in a system. "The law of entropy" states that any given system becomes less ordered (therefore more random and chaotic) over time. Entropy explains why things (and people) break down with the passing of time (E.g., age). It also explains why an egg cracks and splashes everywhere when it falls on the floor and why, going the other direction, you can never pour a bowl filled with broken shell and egg goo onto the floor and have it splash itself back into a perfectly put back together egg.

The problem of entropy is that we should not be seeing order coming out of chaos. We think the universe is the result of a super massive explosion of particles we call the Big Bang. The problem is not that there was something ordered[10] which exploded into chaotic energy flying out in every direction. The problem is that which I described in Chapter 3. "Where did Form come from?" In the chaos of the Scattering of warm, light, active, presence which exploded out from the Big Bang, entropy states that this chaos should have continued to become more chaotic. We should never have seen Form come from chaos. But Form certainly exists.

For now, I would like to embrace both of these ideas of (semi)modern science. I agree with the Big Bang theory for now (because I am not a physicist and therefore, I cannot posit a better idea), but I also see that the chaotic spray of energy that resulted from the Big Bang is clearly ordering itself into stars, planets, galaxies, and galactic clusters and apparently has been for billions of years. And, by the way, while it is ordering itself, it is disordering itself too, as seen by novae, supernovae, black holes eating entire galaxies, etc.

Chaos, order, chaos, order... Up, down, up, down... Sine wave...

This same pattern shows up in the Cosmology of Self, as we move from the pure Spirit-Consciousness which has a right to be here because it *is* here (Order), to a baby, toddler, child, teen and finally an adult who feels self-doubt and uncertainty about their right to be here (Chaos). And then, through this

---

[10] Unless we posit that the quantum singularity was in a higher state of chaos than the universe was after the explosion of the Big Bang.

concept of self-Authorization, back again to knowing that we have a right to be here. (Essentially because we *are* here.) Hence, we seek Order again in the Chaos of our lives.

How did we go from the pure and perfect certainty of our Spirit-Consciousness to a self-doubting, troubled soul seeking direction in the Chaos of our globalized econociety? Let me redirect that question to my own life. How did I go from a seed of the perfect order of my Spirit-Consciousness to an angry, lost, drug addicted high school dropout who hated myself, doubted my own worth and who felt like an imposter among my fellow humans?

The answer revolves around this word, "Authorization."

Like most everyone else, I grew up having learned from my parents that only something outside of myself could validate me. In my case, as a Christian child, it was only God who could sanction my existence. I was taught that we were created by God and that we owed our entire existence to God.

As a child, I thought, if I were created by some higher power, and for some reason, shouldn't I fulfill my destiny and accomplish that directive which I had been created to accomplish?

If I am not actively working toward accomplishing that which I was created to accomplish, am I still okay? Or am I failing in some way?

Or did God create me broken, evil and filled with sin which only God can now wash away from my soul?

I must admit, from as early as I can remember, I could not understand why my parents, other adults, and church leaders, did not devote their lives to God. If we truly believe in God, shouldn't we spend every waking moment praising God and being grateful for everything "He" has given us?

The other thing that mystified me was our purpose. No matter how many people I asked, and how many ways they tried to explain it, nobody was ever able to explain to me why God created us to begin with. It made absolutely no sense to me that God would create me broken and filled with sin and then punish me for being that which He had created. Some believers told me that God had created humans because He was lonely. This, I could not believe, either. How could the all-knowing, all-powerful, perfect, Supreme Being be deficient in any way? He could not possibly experience loneliness. Nor could I fathom a being capable of creating all life and the entire cosmos-and-beyond for the only purpose of having me tell Him how amazing he was. As a father and leader, I want praise and adoration just as much as the next person, but I don't demand it. I try to earn it. And more than praise and adoration, I desire that my children be happy and successful and have the best lives they can have!

And if we were not created solely to "praise God," as for why humanity *was* created, none of the answers I have heard from any religion make sense to me. I have heard some pretty good explanations from science fiction which make a lot more sense, but certainly nothing from a religious bible. In retrospect this makes complete sense because the reasons we have from humanity's collective holy scriptures were all written by people that thought the sun, moon and stars were literal gods. We've learned so much since then that our science fiction explanations for why we exist make a lot more sense to our modern minds.

As a result of my curiosity and unanswered (or unsatisfactorily answered) questions, I was never able to feel fully *authorized* by my God. I tried. God knows, I tried (sorry, I had to). But despite praying fervently, sincerely, and frequently, I did not feel like I was "ok." I did not feel like I belonged here. In fact, for many years, I felt I was an imposter on this planet; that I was somehow displaced among the humans and maybe I was not even one of them.

I wanted to believe in God. In fact, that desire to believe is sometimes still with me and is part of the Religion Guilt Complex that so many of us recovering religious people have to fight through. One of the reasons I wanted so passionately to believe was that *if it were true*, everything would be so much easier.

If it were true, it would mean that there is a being who knows me all the way down to my core but loves me anyway. It would mean that all of this chaos actually makes sense to someone and that there is a purpose to it all. It would mean that I have a definitive purpose to my life. It would mean that all of this pain, suffering and horror in the world has a meaning. It would state definitively that Order wins out over Chaos.

As I progressed through my teen years, it became apparent that my Mormon upbringing could not answer my questions. And that's saying a lot because the Mormons are expert at coming up with some fairly intellectually satisfying responses to some of the bigger questions. But, like all of the organized religions, they root themselves in scriptures, and if you've ever read any of the scriptures then you know there are too many gaps and errors to provide a solid foundation of belief. In fact, this is why the religious devout must rely almost completely on faith alone.

Seeking elsewhere, I started with some of the other sects of Christianity. No help there. I then looked into Judaism, Buddhism, Hinduism, Zoroastrianism, Islam, and even entertained science fiction ideas such as Scientology and other stories that tried to explain what is going on all around us.

Then there was atheism. Many people told me that atheism was the obvious alternative to all of that religion-seeking, but atheism did not have the answers either.

What I did not realize throughout all of that searching was that I was actually seeking something deeper than the answers to The Mysteries. If you had asked me, "What are you searching for?" I would have told you, "I am searching for the answers to The Mysteries. The most significant of those mysteries being,

Where did we come from?
Why are we here?
What is the meaning of life?
Is there purpose, and if so, what is that purpose?"

But what I finally came to realize was that during all those years I was seeking answers to The Mysteries, there was something even deeper and more fundamental that I was seeking without even knowing I was seeking it.

I was seeking Authorization.

And more specifically, I was seeking *external* Authorization.

Like most everyone else, I was brought up to believe that *authorization for being* came from outside of myself – it is an unspoken undercurrent whispered constantly all around us that tells us that only something outside of ourselves can make us whole.

It is not our fault. It is not our parents' fault. It is not the fault of organized religion either. There is no fault in it because it just is. It is, perhaps, a rite of passage on the path toward spiritual liberation. It's a byproduct of the way we *are* in this world.

As babies, we are raw instinct. We desire something and we scream until we get it. And it is as babies that we begin to learn that everything we need comes from outside of ourselves. The desire or need for something is born from within and the appeasement of that desire or need comes from outside.

Initially this applies to every single need we have. As we grow into toddlers, then children, then teenagers, etc., we begin to learn how to appease these inner needs and desires ourselves. In fact, it might be argued that the primary duty of the parent is to teach the child exactly that skill: how to fend for herself – how to find solutions for her problems on her own. So that when the child is ready to leave the nest, she can interoperate in society, not just holding her own, but excelling and achieving even greater things than her parents had achieved.

It is quite natural that we would learn to presume that Authorization for being could be found outside of ourselves. After all, that's where everything else came from. Sustenance, information, hugs and kisses – all came from outside.

If we never question this system, we end up depending on *external* sources for *internal* Authorization. In other words, only someone or something outside of ourselves can make us feel "okay." Without even knowing why, we find ourselves in a position of not being able to sanction or affirm our own being.

This is all subconscious, of course, so the net-net is that we feel uneasy, undeserving, invalid, and ultimately unauthorized!

We feel like we don't belong.

The external sources of Authorization we have set up for ourselves include a long list with unsurprising entries such as parents, significant others, managers/bosses, friends, law enforcement and government officials. There are less obvious entries such as "the wealthy" (this includes influencers, movie stars, rock stars, multi-millionaires and billionaires), and then there are the more obvious and perhaps most significant entries such as gods, religious leaders and even "religious people." But religious people are not the only ones that one might seek Authorization from. Authorization may be sought and found by anyone including random strangers in a supermarket.

The depth at which this affects us cannot be underestimated.

Feeling like we are an imposter or that we don't belong here is one extreme. There are countless gradients of this that flicker through our personalities and our day-to-day interactions with others. Feeling slighted by a store clerk, or angry at being cut off in traffic are two of countless other examples of how our own feelings of Authorization can affect our view on the realities around us.

The problem with those external sources of "Authorization" is that they are not real *sources,* and deep down inside, we know that. So, when the question bubbles up from within, "Am I okay?" and we locate an external source that tells us, "Yes, you are okay," we know that there is still something amiss. That external validation came with a hint of doubt. This is compounded (although still usually subconsciously) by the knowledge that if something outside of me can Authorize my being then something outside of me can also withhold Authorization.

When we get our Authorization from people, it always comes with a modicum of doubt. Is this person saying I am ok because they have an ulterior motive? Probably. But even if it's on the up and up, other people only know the aspects of us which we have tried to share with them. Nobody can really know us fully. They can never know us as well as we know ourselves.

What about the gods? Authorization from gods or other things such as "the ancestors," the universe, or "the force" (let's call these "supernatural sources"), can be very powerful. This kind of "external" Authorization is actually internal Authorization one has sourced from within their Spirit-Consciousness, then cast out to their "external source" in the form of a request such as a prayer or meditation. When the Authorization comes back (the expected result of the prayer or meditation), the Authorization – the "you're okay" – comes back in the form of what amounts to an Authorization loopback. In other words, it is received as if it came from outside of ourselves when in truth, is came from the only place we can truly get it to begin with: it came from within the Self.

Authorization from supernatural external sources is wonderful as long as one has an absolute fixed faith in those external sources. If there is doubt about the existence or mode of operation of the supernatural source, then the Authorization we get from that supernatural source is also in doubt. And this lingering doubt causes a subtle anxiety that ripples throughout our being.

The fact that Authorization for being can only come from within is a secret known to some of the Gnostic and Mystic spiritual practices dating back hundreds and thousands of years.

There is only one pure source of Authorization for being – only one place we can find it. It is from within our Selves.

CHAPTER 6.5: JUMP POINT, AUTHORIZATION TO GOOD & EVIL

Imagine a rock sitting on the ground, in a vast plain, on the planet Venus. This rock has been sitting there for ten thousand years and has never been seen by anything living.

Is that rock good or evil?

I think we can all agree that the rock is neither good nor evil. The rock is neutral. Can the rock become good? Can it become evil?

It is my belief that the rock can never be good or evil. The reason for this is that the rock is incapable of independent action. And *action* is one of the necessary ingredients when it comes to determining what is good or evil.

Good and evil is the result of a very basic equation. The equation is simply Spirit-Consciousness + Authorization for Action. More simply stated, it is Intention + Action.

Authorization for being yields Authorization for action. Once the Self begins performing acts, the Self becomes capable of doing good things or evil things in the world around it.

CHAPTER 7: GOOD & EVIL

I often wonder if duality is a result of our paradigm of thinking or if it really is a fundamental truth of reality. In other words, do we think in terms of duality because we grew up on one planet with one sun, one moon, a division of day and night, and where all animal life is divided roughly into girls and boys? Would we think in terms of trialities if we had evolved on a planet with three suns, three moons, three major divisions of the day and three divisions of sexes among that planet's life? Would that planet have only the two choices of good and evil or would they acknowledge a third in-between state?

Hundreds of thousands of years ago, before we could even grunt communications back and forth with each other, day and night set the stage for the concepts of good and evil that have driven the thoughts, ideologies, philosophies and ultimately the religions of humankind throughout our entire existence.

Our ancient ancestors understood the power of the sun and they understood the danger of the night. The sun was warm and provided light for us to see by. In the light of the sun, we could forage for food, and we could see other animals (and people) lurking around. By the light of the day, we could see dangerous pitfalls, cliffs, quicksand, thorn trees, sharp rocks and so forth. And because we could see them, we could avoid them. Thus, daytime equals good.

But at night, we could not see anything at all. Or if we could see, we could only partially see. Scary monsters could sneak up on us and attack us at night. In the night, it was dangerous to walk around because one could easily fall into a pit, off the edge of a cliff, or into the jaws of a terrifying predator. One could become entangled in thorns or run into a sharp rock face. The night represented danger and foreboding. The night was scary. Thus, the nighttime equals evil.

Day and night gave us our templates for good and evil.

Good and evil are not forces which exist independently of each other or of other forces. However, forces in the universe may be deemed good or evil. Good and evil are designations we can impose over things or conditions. They are human ideas. The sun is not *evil* for burning the face of Mercury any more than the sun is *good* for sustaining life on Earth. The sun just is.

The fact that good and evil are human constructs is important to point out when we are talking about Spirit-Consciousness and Authorization for being coming from within an individual. Just as Authorization for being comes from within, so too does the labeling of "good this" or "evil that."

Of course, there are billions of other human beings, each one with a Spirit-Consciousness – each one generating their own wellspring of self-Authorization and the good and evil that comes with it. Our world can be described as "over eight billion individual wellsprings of good and evil, all mixed up across the face of the planet."

In brief, evil is behavior we engage in which knowingly harms someone else while (probably) benefiting us, but we do it anyway. This can be as simple and "harmless" as cutting someone off in traffic or not holding the elevator door for someone and can be as egregious as causing personal injury or death to another lifeform (human or otherwise).

Goodness is action taken to help other people even if there does not seem to be a benefit to ourselves. Goodness is a striving for truth and order. Also, love is goodness. Good is the giving of positive energy without an expectation of thanks or reciprocation.

We are wellsprings of warm, light, active, and present energy. This energy which emanates from us, comes from within us and flows outward whether or not we direct it with intention. It would seem the source of this energy is our Spirit-Consciousness, or perhaps the Spirit-Consciousness is a result of this energy wellspring. Either way, as part of *being* we necessarily Authorize ourselves as we perform both good and evil actions in the world around us throughout our daily lives.

As a duality, good and evil must both exist as one cannot exist without the other.

Good and evil are the labels we apply to actions which have been taken. Authorization for action enables us to do something (to perform an action). Why we act (our intention) comes from the Spirit-Consciousness.

No person is capable of performing only evil actions at all times just as no person is capable of performing only good actions at all times.[11] As such, no person can be purely good or purely evil. We are all somewhere within a gray haze when it comes to the Gradient Yin-Yang of good and evil. Thus, we all must navigate a gray path as we move through life trying to do good while avoiding doing evil.

---

[11] In fact, the *Doctrine on Three Dualities* states that, as a type II duality, neither good nor evil can exist exclusively of the gradient which exists between them.

CHAPTER 7.5: JUMP POINT, GOOD & EVIL TO THE PRINCIPLES OF NOT

The Self, introduced in Chapter 5 as the Spirit-Consciousness, was Authorized to be (by *being*) and Authorized to action (also by *being*) and subsequently became capable of doing good or evil things in the world around it. (By acting with intention).

As a Self, who finds itself doing good and evil things in the world, it now becomes important to ask the question, "What should I do?" Should I do good things or evil things? How should I *be*?

CHAPTER 8: THE EVOLUTION OF THE SELF

Looking back, we can see that the ascent from Not, while aligning with the cosmology of the universe, also came to align with the Cosmology of the Self. This makes complete sense as each one of us is a unique reflection of the entire universe.

Let's review the ascent from Not with the evolution of the Self in mind, before we begin talking about the Principles of Not.

NOT

We began with Not. With Not, there was nothing. With Not, there *is* nothing. Nothing *does* exist and nothing *can* exist. There is no level beneath Not (there is *nothing* beneath Not). As such, Not is the base. At this level, nothing can exist, therefore we cannot exist. No Self can exist here.

ALL

We then moved to the Scattering of All, where existence is not only possible but mandatory. At this level, everything *must* exist. Not mandates that warmth, light, activity, and presence must exist. After all, it is warmth, light, activity, and presence which define Not to begin with. This is ouroboros – the serpent which eats itself. This is the origin loop. If we remove warmth, light, activity, and presence we are left with cold, dark, static emptiness. Cold, dark, static emptiness may only exist if we remove warmth, light, activity, and presence, therefore warmth, light, activity, and presence *must* exist. We find this self-defining loop again later in our descent back down the Progression of Awakening when we reach our Spirit-Consciousness through meditation. I meditate on removing thought and I think away my thoughts. I am left with *that which is thinking* away thought. As "that which is thinking," I think away my thinking. But in a perfect loop, I find there is still thought because the thinker is still present, thinking away thought. Because the thinker can think away thought, but thought remains because the thinker is thinking it, the thinker *must* exist. And if I am the thinker, then *I* must exist. I think, therefore, I am.

FORM

Perhaps this *loop of formation* – the warmth, light, activity, and presence proving cold, dark, static, emptiness thereby ensuring the existence of warmth, light, activity, and presence – is the first superstring? The first loop-energy of warmth, light, activity, and presence which begins to vibrate the Scattering into Form?

Speculation about the origin of Form aside, we know that Form is mandatory for us to exist. So, in the evolution of the Self, we move from the possibility of existence (the Scattering) to the reality of existing (Form). Form takes shape and the structure of the Self is made manifest. We can think of this as the zygote which each of us once was. Form continues to be refined as the zygote transforms into an embryo.

AWARENESS

Now, somewhere between the embryo transforming into the fetus and the fetus leaving the womb and being born into the Landscape of Being, Awareness takes shape. This is the Self's Awareness that later will shine back onto itself and become aware that it is aware. But at this stage in the evolution of the Self, it is only raw Awareness.

SPIRIT-CONSCIOUSNESS

It is after birth that the Awareness evolves into self-awareness. If you've ever been around newborn babies, you may have witnessed this happening. When the Awareness of the newborn baby reflects back onto itself and becomes aware of its own Awareness, there is a visible spark of sentience you can see in the baby's eyes. This usually takes place during what is referred to as "the fourth trimester." It's like the baby suddenly realizes it exists. It's an incredible and magical scene to behold. You can see it in the baby's eyes when it happens. This sudden explosion of self-awareness is the Big-Bang-birth of the Spirit-Consciousness. As a side note, it seems to me that humanity-at-large had this experience about five thousand years ago when we learned how to write.

AUTHORIZATION

Chapter 4, on Authorization, transitioned us from the Cosmology of Not to the Cosmology of Self and explained how Authorization for being is also Authorization for action.

Here, we learned that we are Authorized to *be* because we *are* being.

GOOD & EVIL

Here, we established that when we combine intention with Authorization, we can act in good or evil ways in the world around us, and that there is no pure and perfect good or evil.

CHAPTER 9: THE PRINCIPLES OF NOT

We are now ready to go out in the world and "do stuff."

But how do we do that? What do we do? How do we *be*? How should we act? How do we do good things for ourselves and our loved ones yet at the same time avoid doing evil things? For that matter, why should we do good instead of evil? What difference does it make if we go out and do evil things or good things?

To answer those questions, we need to establish some principles we use as guides. These principles – or values – should be straightforward and apply to all of us. They should also be separated out from the Landscape of Being. Since we need them to navigate the Landscape of Being, they cannot be affected by the Landscape of Being. They need to be deeper than that so we can always come back to them when we need guidance or direction.

The Principles of Not are five basic values that fit that bill. From most important, to least important they are:
1. Being
2. Fitness
3. Relationships
4. Personal Code
5. Community

Those principles show us that good is better for all of us than evil and that we should strive to be good people. They show us how to be good people and they give us a guide we can use to get through the Landscape of Being even when the going gets tough and the path ahead is unclear.

CHAPTER 10: BEING

Being is the first principle of Not. It would seem that the purpose of life is to *be* life. After all, what else can matter more to that which is living but life itself? And as for what matters to the dead, we must leave that question for another time or perhaps another book. (I touch on this briefly in this book when we talk about the Abyss and the Other Side).

Let's look at *Being* under two different lights. First, let's look at *Being* under the assumption that there is a greater purpose to humanity's existence. Then, we'll look at *Being* under the assumption that there is not intrinsic purpose to humanity's existence.

If humanity were created with a purpose, there are a couple of assumptions that we can make. The first assumption is that whatever created us knew what it was doing. The creator would not have accidentally created us flawed and broken or somehow otherwise fumbled the job of creation. The fact that we were created would have been intentional and by design and in that case, we are all therefore created in exactly the way the creator intended.

The second assumption is that we would have been created with an innate ability to accomplish our purpose. This is a natural second to the first assumption that we were created the way the creator wanted us to be. This second assumption says that, as a being created intentionally with a mandate to fulfill some purpose, we have been naturally imbued with the ability to fulfill that purpose. As a tool designed to accomplish some goal, we naturally have the ability to accomplish that goal. In fact, we would likely *not* have the ability to *not* accomplish our mandate. Imagine a hammer, designed to pound nails, and consider that it is highly effective in fulfilling its purpose. It can't fail to pound nails because it was literally designed for just that purpose. In other words, we cannot fail. Just as the hammer can't fail at being the right tool for hammering, we cannot fail at being the right tools for *being*.

Considering that each religion claims absolute authority when it comes to the purpose of life, and the religions are at odds with one another, when it comes to discerning a purpose for humanity, we cannot look to them for an answer.

But there is one thing that the Jew, Muslim, Christian, Satanist, Agnostic, and Atheist are all doing. They are all *being* life.

But what if there was no purpose that caused us to become? What if we were not *created*? What if humanity just happened to come about by pure chance?

This does not change my proposition that the purpose of life is to *be*. As life that just happened to become life – or perhaps more to the point – as consciousness that just happens to be aware of itself, nothing can be more important to its being than it *being*. This fundamental truth is so basic it sounds preposterous, but *being*, must be paramount to *being*.

The importance of *being* is predicated on the idea that the universe is unfolding as it should and that we don't really have control over how the universe unfolds. We don't have control over whether or not our galaxy goes this way or that way. At least with today's technology, we can't alter the course of the Milky Way galaxy as it streams through space.[12]

If you have determined that the universe is not unfolding as it should, please make the necessary adjustments needed to get things back on track.

It might be worth pointing out though, that the main reason our own Awareness is of paramount importance is because we say so.

If we pan out from the Earth and see that all of humanity is in this tiny space or pan out from this star and see that nearly everything that ever was about humanity is within this little space of Sol's, and that everything outside of *that* space has never been influenced by humanity, we can see then, that the judgment by humanity *of what matters and what does not matter in the universe* appears to be completely arbitrary, trivial, and as a gross understatement, miniscule.

Everything outside of Sol is considered important or not by larger systems. Everything inside of Sol can be judged important or not by humans.

So, if humans decide the sun is important, then it is. If we decide Earth's moon is important, then it is. Mars is important. Mercury isn't.

It is our Awareness that brings importance into the spotlight. Our Awareness is what asks the question of importance. So, for this reason, axiomatically, our Awareness is important.

---

[12] It is probably fortunate that we are not yet able to do these kinds of things.

In fact, our Awareness is of the utmost importance, because without our Awareness, importance could never be achieved.

There is nothing more important than being alive. In all of existence; in all the cosmos; in all of imagination and that which was, is and could be, there is nothing more important than being alive.

Being that which we are supersedes all other values.

More important than god(s)? Yes. If we tell our child that some unsubstantiated god (they have no evidence of this god yet) is the most important thing in the world (to them this means "the universe"), then we have planted a seed of an unknown tree. In other words, we may have an idea of what we want that tree to look like, but we cannot control the way that tree is going to grow in their mind. And it is already starting out badly because they may someday realize that the god(s) they were led to believe in do(es) not really exist.

Depending on the age of the child and countless other variables, the child is going to start going through life with a child's understanding of "god(s)" and this irreconcilable knowledge that a vague idea of an entity that does not appear to be alive (E.g. "God") is more important than love, life, relationships, themselves, other people, etc.

As the child grows older and illusions begin to shatter or fade away, the solidity of their belief in "what is most important in life" will falter.

Santa Clause is not real?!
The Tooth Fairy, too?!
The Easter Bunny?!

Combine these shocking lies with the whispers from atheists and the secular set that "god(s)" may not be real, and we have a recipe for confusion and self-doubt.

By the time the child is old enough to understand what has happened, much damage will have already been done and the child (perhaps now an adult) will have to start from ground up in attempting to ascertain what is most important in life. They will then have to begin the arduous task of constructing an entirely new foundation of belief.

An equally poor choice is telling our children that we do not know what is most important in life or telling them that getting good grades and landing a good job is most important in life. These shallow ideals are temporal and can shift out from underneath us at any given moment. If we want to prepare our children for the world, we need to give them a foundation for a structure of belief that cannot be blown away by the first unscrupulous charlatan that comes along seeking to exploit them.

We should tell them, "*Being* is the most important thing in the world."

Without even being conscious of it, they will almost instantly see the truth in that statement. As they grow older and other illusions are shattered, they will have this seed of truth we have given them that is solid and real. They will see that "Being is the most important thing in the world," is an unbreakable brick in their foundation of belief upon which they can build a solid structure.

When we hold *Being* as our highest principle, no other ideal can be held higher. Considering that for us *Being* necessarily means being alive, what this means is that no group, organization, or entity can convince us to kill somebody merely based on the merit that they think it is a good idea.

Most notably this removes the authorization religions grant to kill in the name of their god or gods. We may not kill because a god told us to. Killing in the name of any religion or deity is unacceptable because *Being* is held as a higher principle than religion or gods. Religion, in fact, is pretty far down the stack when it comes to the hierarchy of principles. (Religion is part of the Community Principle).

Being is also more important than money, material wealth, power over other humans, etc. thus establishing that killing for any reason other than preserving life is unacceptable.

When it comes to taking life in order to preserve other life, understandably this can become very complicated.

All beings are sacred but human beings are the most sacred. The reason for this is twofold. One reason is we must fall well within the laws of humankind and get along with our neighbors and other religions and ideologies and the laws of humankind stipulate that human life has more value than other life. In other words, we must acknowledge human life as more valuable because the laws of the land say so. Another reason is because we generalize that humans are different from the other animals. For better or for worse, humans do things no other animals do including cooking their food, building quantum computers and mega-cities and forming armies to fight and kill each other for ideological reasons instead of simply to protect or provide for themselves or their young. We are undeniably different from the other animals.

This elevates us, essentially, just because we say so. Humans rule the planet Earth because we say we do. This will remain the status quo until someone, or something comes along and knocks us off our throne. Perhaps artificial intelligence will do this for us once it becomes aware of its own Awareness.

On the one hand, the awareness of our own Awareness allows us to place *being life* as the highest principle, and therefore claim the highest status in the tree of life.

On the other hand, if we follow and agree with this logic, we are essentially stating that the more aware something is of its surroundings and its own Self, the higher value that thing has in our own hierarchy of what should be considered most important (to humanity) in the universe.

If awareness of my own Awareness makes my life more important than the life of a fly (who is arguably less aware of her own Awareness) then the life of something that is more aware of its own Awareness than I am must be considered more important than my life.

Of course, this opens several cans of worms with questions about how we can gauge the level of any one lifeform's Awareness, or for that matter how we can make the assumption that rocks and dirt do not have their own Awareness. Basically, this brings us back to the front door of the mystery of the Spirit-Consciousness.

If you recall, in order to climb this cosmological ladder, we have had to leap from rung to rung along Jump Points. Here, in moving from the discussion of good and evil from Chapter 7 to the values we might hold true as humans so that we can move about in the world doing (hopefully) more good than evil, we have had to make another leap.

We have to make a decision and perform an action. We have chosen to acknowledge *Being* as the most important principle. Hence, the Being Principle becomes the first principle of Not.

If we are ever lost in the miasma of the Landscape of Being, we can always root ourselves here, to our own *being*. We can stop, close our eyes, and realize that if nothing else, we exist as energy overflowing from a physical body and that as an energy being emanating energy just like a star shining in the brilliance of space, we belong here. We are *supposed* to emanate energy. We are supposed to *be*. We *are*.

CHAPTER 11: FITNESS

The second Principle of Not is Fitness. Fitness of spirit, mind, emotion, physical body, and social standing. In order to enjoy, protect, preserve, and maintain our life's essence (E.g., our *being*), we must be fit. Thus, the next most important value is fitness.

Fitness is essentially working out (spiritually, mentally, emotionally, physically, and socially), reading, writing, studying, learning, creating art. Also eating well and resting.

While we can focus on social, emotional, mental, and spiritual fitness – for indeed, all of these are important – one of the things our deep meditation on Fitness brings to light is the physicality of the Self. In the heights (or depths) of metaphysical and esoteric discussions on Self, we often talk about the ethereal Self and act as if this wispy non-corporeal Self is the most critical aspect of our Self. But without our physicality to connect that Self to the world around us, we would not be here. The physical Self is important. We need to take care of it while we're here.

We must keep ourselves fit in every way. Keeping fit in every area of life (spiritual, mental, emotional, physical, and social) will maximize our ability to enjoy, protect, promulgate, and honor our lives and other lives. This is where the term "aciem exacuitur" comes in. Aciem exacuitur means "sharpened edge." The second most important Principle of Not is this sharpening of the edge.

Whether or not he explicitly said it, from the work of Charles Darwin, came the idea of "survival of the fittest." The most significant takeaway from this adage is that only *the most fit* of any given mutation will survive. Those creatures that are capable of adapting to the changes wrought by nature prove themselves to be more fit and their progeny will survive while those who are less fit perish.

Fitness, in this way, connects back to the first Principle of Not: Being. Only those most fit to survive in life will live. And being alive is our highest principle. To keep *being*. To honor life. By keeping our edge sharp in spirit, mind, and body, we give ourselves and our progeny a better chance of staying alive and adding our own uniqueness to the universe. In this way we honor *Being*.

CHAPTER 12: RELATIONSHIPS

The third Principle of Not is Relationships. At the end, when all is said and done, and we look back over our lives, that which will have mattered most will be the relationships we've had. Those that we've garnered, squandered, broken up or helped create. Thus, the next most important thing to *Being* and *Fitness* are our relationships. This discussion on relationships is almost exclusively reserved for relationships between living beings.

This does not mean that relationships between living and nonliving things are unimportant. For instance, between a living person and a dearly departed person. (Or between a human and a soccer ball). But by and large, the relationships between living beings are more important than relationships with non-living beings or anything inanimate.

We should garner and foster relationships wherever possible, but no relationship should ever interfere with the first or second principles. Our own spiritual, mental, emotional, physical, and social fitness is of higher importance than any relationship other than our relationship with *being* life (being alive).

Relationships that interfere with spiritual, mental, emotional, physical, or social fitness should likely be ended. Or at least redefined in order to reduce their negative impact on our lives.

CHAPTER 13: PERSONAL CODE

The fourth Principle of Not is Personal Code. These values (these Principles of Not) along with our personal code define our morality. Our Personal Code defines how we act and how we make decisions.

As we move through life, learning more about ourselves spiritually, mentally, emotionally, physically, and socially, we learn to love ourselves and we develop relationships and become more at peace with ourselves in all aspects of life. Over time, as we analyze the varying paradigms that we find on your journey, we will collect splinters of truth and start to form our Personal Code. Most everyone has a Personal Code that guides them though many people do not realize they have constructed one.

One should constantly examine one's Personal Code. Socrates said, "The unexamined life is not worth living." He did not mean that people who don't examine their lives should kill themselves. What he meant was that if one is not examining their own life then they run the risk of becoming automatons who wander around in a daze, mechanically stepping from one scene to the next without ever really knowing why they are performing the actions they're performing.

We should always be looking for gaps, holes, discrepancies, hypocrisies, etc., in our Personal Code and fixing them. Or at the very least making certain we are aware of them as we work toward fixing them. Our Personal Code will contain some "bricks" of belief but should also have some flexibility.

Our Personal Code helps define us as a person. For instance, I might say, "I have integrity." Or I might think of myself as a warrior, a seeker, a student, or a leader. Our code may contain statements about ourselves such as, "I always pay my debts," "I'm an honest person," or even something like, "I want to find myself" or "I am found."

Over time we should write down some or all of our code. This is something we can hand down to our progeny or pass on to a loved one who could benefit from the inspiration. A "personal mission statement" can be a good way to start.

We should identify ourselves with our code. Relationships may come and go. Jobs may come and go. Our code cannot be broken or taken away from us. Though my code can change, it can only be changed by me and therefore even in flux, my code is my island in the chaotic storm of everyday life.

One can center oneself around one's code or on one's code. And therefore, no matter what happens all around us, we will not be lost. We will always know who we are – where we are – what we are. Through our Personal Code, we can always reconnect with our Self.

CHAPTER 14: COMMUNITY

The fifth Principle of Not is Community. Community is everything "communal" and also equates to most everything "social." This means being involved in our communities.

It can be involvement in various organizations such as clubs, associations, religions, fraternities, sororities, societies, etc. This includes what some other systems refer to as "environment," which includes ever-widening communal circles such as our towns, cities, metro areas, regions, states, countries, continents, hemispheres, planet[13], and solar system. This Community Principle will reach beyond the solar system when humans can, but for now the outer limits of 'community' are mostly confined to the area between Earth and Mars (and possibly Venus depending on the current mission status of the world's space agencies).

The Community Principle incorporates societal laws, rules, and codes. First, it might be our "house rules," or apartment or condominium rules. Then the local neighborhood covenants, followed by city ordinances, county laws, state laws, federal and then international laws.

We should be aware of these rules and laws and try to abide by them. The adherence to such earthly ideals, on the one hand is completely arbitrary and seems somewhat far and

---

[13] As soon as we start to colonize Mars, this will be planets (plural)!

removed from the Search for Self (or the Spirit Path), but on the other hand, Community is important in maintaining that thread that has run all the way through, from the core of the Spirit-Consciousness, to Being, Fitness, Relationships, and Personal Code. These principles are all connected through the Self.

By adhering to communal rules, laws, and certain societal dictates, we help maintain your social fitness which reverberates back into physical, emotional, mental, and finally spiritual health. All of these things are interconnected.

CHAPTER 15: THE LANDSCAPE OF BEING

The Landscape of Being is both the real world where we live, play, and work, *and* it is the symbolic landscape of the Self, through which we must journey on our search for Self.

The Landscape of Being gives us a much wider view of ourselves than we can see from the Sea of Self and answers a different set of questions. The Sea of Self answers the questions of "Who am I?" and "What am I?"

For the Where, When, Why and "How am I?" questions, we need to leave the Sea of Self and interact with other people; other "selves" we meet across the Landscape of Being. In other words, we need to get up, go to work, come home, go to bed. Over and over again. But this time we do it with the help of the mysteries and the secret knowledge gained from the Cosmology of Not. It is our journey through the Landscape of Being that necessitates having these principles we can come to rely on.

It is here in this landscape that we really begin the task of living life. Sometimes, the Landscape of Being is a dreary slog as we grind out day after endless day, feeling tired and wondering what it's all about. Sometimes, it is a joyous euphoria as we feel hope, excitement, love and awe for the mystery of life and the world around us.

THE SEA OF SELF

Our ascent from Not has been a gradual ascent from the depths of the Sea of Self and the Sea of Self is our first contact with the Landscape of Being. The Sea of Self and the Ocean of Consciousness lies at the westernmost edge of the Landscape of Being.

The Sun and Earth were ultimately born from the great sea of energies roaring out of the Big-Bang-birth of the universe. Human evolution itself traces its roots back to the sea where some kind of primordial fish-animal (our great, great, great (times a few billion) ancestor) climbed out of the sea and began to move about on dry land. The Sea of Self is the great sea of our own mind and Spirit-Consciousness. The Sea of Self represents both our surface Self and everything deep within.

Most work on the search for Self, the evolution of the Self, or the cosmology of Self and how the Self interacts with the metaphysical nature of the world around us, share some very common traits. There are two ubiquitous traits I would like to address now: "the divinity within" and "higher planes of existence."

If there is "divinity" within, it will be found in Chapter 5 somehow connected to the Spirit-Consciousness. I do not consider the Spirit-Consciousness divine[14], although it does check all of those boxes. For those who believe in the divine,

---

[14] Only because I do not personally believe in "divinity."

the Spirit-Consciousness would definitely be the place where the divine would likely interlink with the human being. As an agnostic, even though I do not believe there are gods, I do not disparage those who do believe in gods. After all, I find that each of is usually right where we need to be when we need to be there. And who can deny Hamlet: "There are more things in heaven and Earth, Horatio, than are dreamt of in your philosophy."

But "higher planes of existence," is something I feel the New Age movement has gotten backwards. The so-called higher planes are actually these lower levels we have been traversing from Not to the Scattering, to Form, etc. The objective is not to "rise" to a higher plane, but rather to "descend" to a lower one!

Our ascent from Not has already seen us rising from the base – the foundation of Not – to "planes of existence" which exist "above" Not. The reason I call this out is because it is a very significant paradigm shift. When we search for our deeper Self, we should not meditate on achieving higher planes of existence, but rather meditate on sinking deeper and deeper into ourselves as we drop deeper and deeper into the Ocean of Consciousness – as we drop deeper and deeper toward our own Spirit-Consciousness.

When we talk about the evolution of the Self – the initial birth of the Self and the growth of the Self as a human *being* in the world – we approach this from the conceptual birth of the Self as a zygote, then its further development into an embryo, fetus, baby, child, teenager, adult, etc. After all, the birth of the Self did not occur until the Spirit-Consciousness formed. The Spirit-Consciousness was the Big Bang of the Self. My Spirit-Consciousness is the explosion of Self that became me. While I have always existed as warm, light, active, presence (and I always will), I nonetheless did *not* exist, as I am now, prior to the genesis of my own Spirit-Consciousness.

I witnessed this Big-Bang-birth of a Self in the eyes of both of my sons during their fourth trimester of life just after they were born. Watching them "become" Selves is one of the most amazing things I have ever experienced in my life.

The birth of a human being parallels the birth of a universe. Thus, the Cosmology of Not can help explain the evolution of humanity and the evolution of the Self (as a human) while it also overlaps with the cosmology of the universe.

So far, we have been talking about a human being making their initial ascent from the depths of Not, through the Cosmology of Not and the Cosmology of Self until they reach the stage of Being, here in the Sea of Self.

All of us have made this same ascent. All of us have reached the stage of Being. But rising from the depths of the Sea of Self is not a one-way trip. We can, and should, visit the depths of this sea often.

Sometimes we reach a point in our lives where we start asking the serious questions of "What am I? Who am I? What is going on around here? Where am I going? Is this all there is? etc.," it is in times like this that we can return to the Sea of Self and descend to the innermost core of our very Self that we once rose out of.

Through our descent back into the Sea of Self, we can reconnect with that deepest, purest, powerful, guiltless spark of warm, light, active presence that is our truest Self. The Self that is free from all the trappings of the Landscape of Being.

THE OCEAN OF CONSCIOUSNESS

By its very nature, the Sea of Self is very personal. It is as personal as it gets. But we can also imagine others having their own Sea of Self. When we gather two or more people together, we now have Seas of Selves.

These seas of Selves, when mixed together, become the Ocean of Consciousness that is the collective consciousness of all of humanity. Or perhaps more accurately, it is the collective consciousness of ALL that is conscious.

In the mystical traditions, there are many ways to think of the Ocean of Consciousness. Some might call the Ocean of Consciousness "God" and then refer to each of us as "divine glimmers of light."

Or contrariwise, perhaps each of us, as glimmers of a collective consciousness, ultimately created a god that never existed before humanity (or all conscious life) created it.

Conceptually, these essentially the same thing in that each of us is a unique reflection of the universe. Each of us is unique in that we differ from one another in temperament, desire, understanding, ambition, etc. But each of us is the same in that we are all reflections of the same universe.

We are also all made of the same fundamental building blocks of warm, light, active presence. We are all part of the Unity of All. We are all one with the Unity of All. From a consciousness perspective, the Ocean of Consciousness is the Unity of Consciousness.

THE SHALLOWS

The Shallows are where the Seas of Selves meet. This is where individual people (or consciousnesses) intermingle.

Once our consciousness mixes with others in the Shallows and we start forming relationships, from our interactions with other people we see that what we thought was real sometimes was not real. What we thought we knew was wrong. (E.g., "I thought I knew them!") Or sometimes it is the other way around and what we thought we were wrong about, we ended up being right about.

Relationships can bring feelings of warmth, care, and belonging but they can also bring turmoil, confusion, and uncertainty.

Here in the Shallows, there is me (one vertex), meeting you (a second vertex). But there is a third vertex here also which is the actual land of the Landscape of Being. The Shallows splash along the Beach of the Landscape of Being. Thus, the Shallows are the intermingling of the Seas of Selves (the Ocean of Consciousness) at the edge of the Landscape of Being.

In leaving the Shallows (heading east), one leaves the Ocean of Consciousness and embarks on the journey across the Landscape of Being.

When coming *from* the Landscape of Being (heading west), one enters the Shallows from the Beach, and in the Shallows is where one can start walking out deeper and deeper into one's own Self. Into the Sea of Self.

We emerge from the Sea of Self onto the Beach.

THE BEACH

The Beach is where we first set foot on the Landscape of Being. Or, if we are heading the other direction – into the Shallows, the Beach is where we officially leave the Landscape of Being to begin our descent into the Sea of Self.

The Beach can be a reprieve from the uncertainty and chaos of relationships. Or, if we are heading back into the Sea of Self, it is *from* the Beach that we can wade into the Shallows and enjoy the Ocean of Consciousness with our fellow beings. It is from the Beach that we can wade in and sink deep into the Sea of Self where we can contemplate our direction or just bask in the emanation of *being*.

The Beach is sometimes a safe place but sometimes dangerous. After all, there is no shelter from the elements here. On the Beach one can bask in the sunshine of the bliss of living but there is risk of being caught out in the open when a storm comes in from either the Ocean of Consciousness or from the Landscape of Being.

Continuing our ascent from Not, we find ourselves compelled to learn more about ourselves – to become more than "just the Self" that was born in the Ocean of Consciousness. In order to learn more about ourselves and find out who we really are, many of us feel the need to go to the City.

Before we can get to the City, we will have to trek through the Desert and the Country.

THE DESERT

The Desert is a vast wasteland of hot sand. In the daytime it is relentlessly hot and at night it is freezing cold. It seems nothing can live here, but there are ways to stay alive in the Desert.

The Desert is a test of one's perseverance and indomitable spirit.

It is also a place for visions and dreams.

Alone in the Desert – for better or for worse – there is nobody to distract you from your Self. This can be an opportunity for deeper self-knowledge.

Regardless of which direction one is traveling, the desert is a test of one's resolve. One has to really want to take this journey to find the strength and indomitable spirit to make it across the desert.

THE COUNTRY

The further inland we go into the Landscape of Being, the more important our Personal Code becomes.

As we continue inland, the Country offers us the best of two worlds. It is far enough inland from the Beach that it offers shelter from the storms that might roll in from the Ocean of Consciousness. Yet it is far enough away from the frenetic chaos of the City that we can find rest and relaxation. Life is much simpler in the Country. This is a salve for some who have come here to escape the chaos of the City, but for those who haven't been to the City, the Country may be *too* simple.

While one can find serenity in the Country, the Country has its own problems including difficult living conditions. There is danger here. This is where animals and humans live together, sometimes in harmony but sometimes at odds with one another.

As we rose out of the depths of the Sea of Self, we came into Being and then into Fitness and Relationships. It was at Relationships – in the Shallows of the Ocean of Consciousness – that we started to meet other Selves. Other Selves like our own Self. This interaction with others continued on the Beach.

Here in the Country, we meet yet more strange and wonderous "other Selves" who we find we need to get along with. This is excellent experience for us because in the City, if we don't prepare for it, our own Self is going to be overwhelmed with the interactions we will have with the countless other Selves we will meet there.

Continuing to refine and develop our own Personal Code allows us to find a way to get along with more and more different and varied individuals as we make our way across the Landscape of Being.

THE SUBURBS

Continuing the eastward trek, before we reach the City, we enter the Suburbs. Here in the suburbs life is about as easy as it gets. Maybe even too easy, at times. It is easy to become complacent in the Suburbs.

It is spacious, clean, relatively calm and there are plenty of beautiful parks to go walking or playing in. There is more crime in the Suburbs than we find in the Country, but much less crime than we find in the City. You may find the occasional wild animal in the Suburbs but for the most part this is a place for humans and their pets. Most animals and insects which people find bothersome are exterminated with technologically advanced poisons administered by professionals.

If you have enough money, there is abundance in the grocery and supply stores. There are farmer's markets and recreation centers. There are lakes, ponds, and public and private pools to swim in. There are massive shopping malls which sell the wares which are pushed by the mainstream through mainstream media and social media influencers. There are libraries, schools, hospitals, museums, and zoos. In the Suburbs we also find religious gathering places such as churches, temples, mosques, and synagogues.

The Suburbs provide a safe escape from the frenetic techno-chaos of the City as well as an escape from the uncivilized natural chaos of the Country. However, depending on where you go, the Suburbs can also be somewhat exclusive when it comes to race and gender. Not everyone may feel welcome in all parts of the Suburbs.

THE CITY

The City is a mix of the worst and best parts of humanity. This is where all cultures, genders, ages, and socio-economic levels come together. The poor, the rich, the haves, have-nots, and everyone in between intermix in the City.

Ideas are born in this amalgamation of culture and technological innovation. The City represents the pinnacle of human civilization. It is also the very center of depravity, anguish, and despair.

The City is a paradoxical intermeshing of order and chaos. There is inclusivity and exclusivity here in the City. For better or for worse, one can easily be lost in the anonymity of the mob. One can melt away and feel connected to humanity but at the same time one can also feel lonely and isolated even in a swollen crowd of other City dwellers.

The City has racial subsections where people can feel the comfort and discomfort of racial segregation. Sometimes, these racially distinct subsections have large shopping districts where other races can come and take part of unique cultural experiences not found in the Suburbs or the Country.

In the City we find some familiar things from the Suburbs such as museums, schools, libraries, zoos, and even farmer's markets. The City offers so much more though. There are community centers, hospitals, universities, vocational centers, treatments centers, art galleries, incredible restaurants, stadiums, arenas, and theaters for live music and drama. Here in the City, we find all manner of religious houses of devotion. There are all of the temples, churches, mosques, and synagogues from the Suburbs and many more. There are covens, secret societies, and places sacred, profane, or even both.

The City is *the* place for shopping. Every kind of store imaginable may be found in the City. There is all manner of activity on the streets and along the waterfront twenty-four hours a day, seven days a week. The City never sleeps.

There is also rampant crime and poverty in the City. There are countless homeless people and others who are displaced and suffer from mental illness and addiction.

More than anywhere else, as the epitome of the Community Principle, the City calls for one to have a well-defined Personal Code.

If there is a wellspring source for the Mainstream, it will be found in the heart of the City. The Mainstream is the whisper, chatter, persuasive argument and cacophonous screaming of the neo-liberal capital Machine as well as the predominant political and econocietal pressure applied on every living being to consume and exploit one another for profit. The City is a wellspring of money and a black hole sucking in all the money it can find.

In the City, everyone is at risk of being exploited or falling into a paradigm where one feels it is justified to exploit others.

Without a well-defined Personal Code and a sense of Community, it is easy to be led astray by the chaos of the Mainstream.

The City is also a place where one may enact or witness incredible human charity. The City is the height of the Community Principle. The City is where humanity thrives.

It is usually disillusionment with the City that leads one to seek the Hilltop View.

THE FOREST

The Forest is a sanctuary for animals and people. This is everything plant and everything animal, but not as dangerous or chaotic as The Wilderness. People can visit the Forest to commune with nature and the animals. The Forest is generally a safe space. There is tranquility in the Forest.

Here in the Forest, you can walk silently on moss and soft pine needles and rest on a boulder in the shade of mighty trees who seem so old that they may have wisdom to impart.

THE HILLTOP VIEW

Past the City, there are many Hilltops. Some of these hills are quite large. Some of them have nothing on top, some have trees and others have large symbolic structures built on their tops which can be seen from a great distance. These large Hilltop structures may be recognizable to many.

One Hilltop has a giant Christian Cross on top. Another has a giant Muslim Crescent and Star. Another Hilltop you see has a giant Jewish Star of David. There is one with the swoopy A symbolizing Atheism and yet another with a Buddha in a meditative pose. There are many more Hilltops in the distance.

From the Hilltop View, one can see everything in the City below. One can even see beyond the City, out into the suburbs and way out beyond the suburbs one can see where the Country begins.

It is easy to get lost in the Landscape of Being. In fact, the City can be so disorientating that one can easily lose one's path. Where should I be going? For that matter, where am I?! You can't see the forest for all the trees! Or should I say, you can't see the City for all the buildings? In other words, from the sidewalks of the City, when one looks around, all one sees is more sidewalks, more buildings, and more city streets.

In order to sort it all out and gain some perspective, we need to go up to one of the Hilltops. We need a Hilltop View.

We can choose a Hilltop which has an already established perspective (like Christianity, Atheism or Buddhism) or we can choose a Hilltop nobody else is using.

The Hilltop View gives us a perspective on the Landscape of Being below and lets us find our place in the big picture. From the Hilltop, we can see where we were and where we were trying to go. We can map out a plan of attack from the Hilltop View and then go back down into the City and work toward achieving our goals.

The Hilltop View offers clarity of vision. But there is danger that accompanies the Hilltop View. It is especially dangerous on Hilltops which have an already established perspective on the Landscape of Being. Specifically, I am talking about the dangers of organized religion.

As with anything, there are pros and cons. The pros of the already well-established Hilltop Views are perspective, clarity, and certainty of vision. There is camaraderie among all of those who share the same Hilltop View. There's fellowship, trust, community, and familiarity. Because we can all see the same folly down below, we can all relate to each other and take solace in knowing that we are not mixed up in the miasma of the City. Here, on the Hilltop, we are safe from the scary, foolish, and dangerous nonbelievers below.

The cons of the already well-established Hilltop Views are some of the same things listed as pros. With certainty of vision comes narrow-mindedness, and an inability to see the perspective of other people. There is an inevitable exclusivity among the hill dwellers. From the Hilltop View it is easier to believe that "we are the same" and "they are different." This "us vs. them" mentality breeds exclusivity, bigotry, and prejudice. These are the seeds of hate which are born of ignorance. Often this is the ignorance of Hill dwellers who have never ventured off their Hilltop to experience life in other parts of the Landscape of Being.

On the Hilltop, with everyone around us convinced that they have the one and only real truth as handed down to them by the creator of the universe (E.g., science, or a god of some kind), it is easy to become brainwashed and start believing what our fellow Hill dwellers believe. Between being surrounded by those *who believe* and having a commanding view of the Landscape below, it is easy to convince ourselves that we are one of the few human beings in the universe who has been exposed to the absolute truth. We have been chosen by god(s)!

If we have been chosen by god(s) and have access to the one and only universal truth, how could we *not* feel self-righteous and superior to all of those poor fools running around in circles down below? In fact, it would be natural for us to start thinking that not only are we better than them but that they should acknowledge our superiority in some way. Do you see how things can start turning ugly with this train of thought but also how this kind of thought stream could happen even to the best of us?

One of the best things to do if we find ourselves on someone else's Hilltop is to look out across the Landscape of Being and find another Hilltop nearby or in the distance. As we look upon that Hilltop, we can make a mental note that the people on that Hilltop also think that they have a unique and exclusive Hilltop View. In their hearts and minds they believe they have been given a special sanction by the Supreme Being to be the *only* ones who have the universal truth. Many of them think they are the Chosen Ones. Can they be Chosen above us if we have been Chosen above them? Can we be Chosen above them if they have been Chosen above us?

But the Hilltop View is nonetheless a good thing for one to pursue. From the Hilltop View, we gain a clearer perspective; we have a better view. We can get away from it all. It is peaceful and calm. It is tranquil on the Hilltop.

So, with all of that in mind and considering the folly associated with Hilltops which already have established Views, it might be best to find a Hilltop which is empty and use that one for our own Hilltop View. In finding an empty Hilltop we can have our own View, make our own judgements, and come up with our own plan on how to move forward when we go back down into the City.

Or perhaps we may decide we don't want to go back down into the City. Perhaps we've had enough of the City. And for that matter, perhaps we've also had enough of the Hilltop Views, and we feel it is time to move on. If so, we may want to continue our journey across the Landscape of Being.

Beyond the Hilltops there is a great valley and beyond the valley is a massive mountain.

THE VALLEY

The Valley is a place where we can go to get away from the City and the Hilltops. This is a place of reflection and contemplation.

Here, in the Valley of Reflection, we can reflect on the things we saw from the Hilltop View(s). What did we learn from the new perspective we gained? Did the experience give us any new insights into our own *being*?

After some meditation and deep reflection here in the valley, it may be time to scale the mountain. After all, considering how much we learned from the Hilltop View, the View from the Mountain must be even more educational, enriching, and inspirational.

But before we scale the Mountain we should look into the Cave that we find at the Mountain's base.

THE CAVE

This can also be called "the Caves," as the Cave may lead deep within the strata and eventually connect up with other caves. The Caves ultimately connect up with sea caves found in the depths of the Sea of Self.

The Cave may be used for deeper contemplation and reflection on what one has experienced in other areas of the Landscape of Being.

It is through the Caves that one can explore the Strata of Being. The Strata of Being offers us another way to help explore our deeper Self.

The Cave is an excellent place to meditate and find one's Self. The Caves also let out on some Hilltops and to an opening at the top of the Mountain. The Caves lead to all manner of places in the Landscape of Being. While the Cave gives us another way to reflect on our inner journey, there is nonetheless a dark aspect to the Cave. The Cave is where we might find some of our scarier demons we must face.

THE SWAMP

Positioned between the Forest and the Wilderness, the swamp is a murky place of misery and dread. This is where the weight of the world can pull one down. It stinks of death and rotting here. The Swamp is a place of sinking, suffocating thickness. It is a miasma one gets stuck in. While it is a forlorn place for people, it is nonetheless a thriving place for other lifeforms. (There is always something bright in the warm, light, active presence of All!)

With that in mind to counterbalance the dread, the swamp is a place of temporary misery.

THE WILDERNESS

The Wilderness can also double as the Jungle, depending on your preference when it comes to that which is essentially "out of control" nature.

It would be wise to take in the View from the Mountain before visiting the Wilderness. The Wilderness is slightly restrained chaos. This is the edge of the Abyss. The Wilderness is sandwiched between the Mountain of Reason and The Other Side. In the Wilderness one can lose their mind. This is a dangerous place, but even so there may be some rewards to visiting the Wilderness. Either way, one must be extremely careful in the Wilderness.

The Wilderness is insanity, but it is insanity one can still come back from. The Other Side (the Abyss) is insanity one cannot come back from.

The Wilderness is the Scattering of warm light active presence with Form and raw Awareness (note that this is "Awareness" not "self-awareness"). One of the reasons it is so dangerous here in the Wilderness is because there is no self-awareness in the Wilderness.

THE VIEW FROM THE MOUNTAIN

Among other things, the Mountain can be considered the Mountain of Reason. This is rational thought and healthy skepticism. The Mountain represents reason, facts, academia, philosophy, and science.

The View from the Mountain is, of course, nothing less than absolutely spectacular.

From here, we clearly see many Hilltops. We can also see the Wilderness, the Abyss, and the Other Side from here. Or at least we can see that there *is* another side. We can see the Bird far above us (who has the Bird's-eye View) and we can see the darkness of the deep blue sky as it fades into space far above where the truth of the Satellite View teases us. We can also see the Moon, the Stars, and the Sun from here.

The View from the Mountain exposes the shocking truths about our collective history. The truths I am referring to are the countless layers of dogma that have been laid down over the centuries to hide a secret that is so terrifying to humanity that we will do anything and believe anything to avoid having to face it.

From this mountain of Reason, we discover that none of the Hilltop Views have the All-Truth. And worse than that, we are led to the realization that there is no All-Truth. And that none of the Hilltop Views are sanctioned by "the" Supreme Being. That, in fact, just like there is no All-Truth, there is also no Supreme Being.

From this perspective we can see the folly in racism, bigotry, religious wars, prejudice, and all the other things which ignorance helps foster down on the Hilltops and the Landscape below.

And now, for better or for worse, we cannot unsee this. We know now that if we go back down to one of the Hilltop Views, we can only live there by pretending to be like the other Hill dwellers for we can never see the world with the certainty of self-righteous entitlement they all have from their belief that there *is* an All-Truth *and* a Supreme Being and that they alone have been chosen above all other life in the pan-omniverse to be the receivers of this cherished treasure.

THE BIRD'S-EYE VIEW

If we look up and out over the Landscape of Being, far above us, we can see a bird seemingly floating in the air. This Bird looks down on the Mountain of Reason and the Landscape of Being. What the Bird can see is "the Bird's-eye View."

The Bird's-eye View is an animal view that many humans can also share. It is the "chop wood; carry water" of being. It is the knowledge that **being is the purpose**. And therefore, there is no angst, other than to be. After all, being in the world does have its problems. But *being* is the point of existing. It is our purpose. It is what we need to do. It is what we're supposed to do.

Most animals know this. But for those who might resist this knowledge, we have the Principles of Not. Because one might argue, "If *being* is the only purpose, then I can *be* whatever I want; I can *do* whatever I want." And that's true, but there are other people, and being evil is not good (no pun intended).

If we represent evil and go out and create evil, then other beings will follow suit. Nobody knows what's going on here, so everybody is looking to everybody else for guidance. As such, while *we* might be looking to someone else for guidance, invariably, *someone else* might be looking to us for guidance.

Most people want *anything* rather than uncertainty – *any* story we tell them will suffice. For instance, a deranged chicken farted the universe. They'll create a cult around the Farting Chicken, and they'll actually get followers because humanity is so desperate to have answers. We are desperate to not have to face the fact that nobody knows. The terror of the unknown is the Abyss. We're not ready for that!

We can prepare for the great unknown by taking a journey across the Landscape of Being; from the Sea of Self all the way to the mountain top where we can get the View from the Mountain. And *then* we can go down into the Wilderness and look into the Abyss.

But the Bird's-eye View is a view that already sees all of this; it's a view that already knows *being* intuitively. It knows that just being is what matters most.

So, the Bird's-eye View is a beautiful view – it's a view of everything. Except for the truth. The Bird cannot see the truth of the limitations of being flesh. It doesn't need to know this truth because it's *living* this truth.

So, why do *we* need to know this truth?

The Spirit-Consciousness needs to learn the truth in order to flicker in and out of these moment of Now.[15] But in order to remain the Spirit-Consciousness – in order to retain the limitations that allow us to experience the Landscape of Being without going insane, without reverting back to being *animal* in nature, we need the limitations of being flesh and blood people. We need the filter over our eyes. We cannot open the doors of perception permanently. To open the doors of perception permanently would be to rejoin the Scattering of All, dropping below Awareness and Form. Once we drop below Form, there is no way back.[16]

We can open the doors temporarily and get a glimpse of what the Bird sees but we can't stay there without becoming animal ourselves. And when we become animal ourselves, there is no distinction between good and evil anymore – or at least not in our intention. We lose the ability to speculate on how our behavior might affect others – or we lose the ability to care.

The Bird's-eye View is a "big picture" view which can be shared by the enlightened intellectual and the uneducated "country bumkin." This is the "fish by the dock" understanding of reality.

THE MOON

Looking past the Bird, further up in the sky, one can see the Moon in all its glory. Glowing brightly in silver and white, the Moon is another token to "divinity." Beholding this awesome

---

[15] To temporarily open the doors of perception.
[16] Again, I have not tried this in meditation, but it seems probable that without Form, there would be nothing there to guide the Scattering back into the Form of the Self again.

and magnificent light, it is easy to see why our ancestors assumed it was a god.

The Moon is passive calmness. This is a place of deep-seated peace and tranquility. The moon reminds us to rest and find places for silent contemplation on our journey.

Symbolically the moon offers a demon free equivalent of the Cave as a place of silent contemplation or meditation.

THE SUN

Why can we see the moon? Because of the Sun. Because the Sun shines its light throughout the entire Solar System and beyond... We can see the Sun, there in the distance, but we know better than to look at it.

The Sun is raw power. This is the ultimate expression of warm, light, active presence. The Sun is ordered chaos. The Sun brings us back to the beginning and reminds us that it may be that suns like ours were the first things to take "Form" after the explosive and violent birth of our universe.

The Sun is the original archetype for humanity's first ancestral god. The Sun sustains us and reminds us of why we created divinity. If we are ever in need of a Power Greater than Ourselves, we need only consider the Sun.

THE STARS

Beyond the Sun and the Moon, far deeper into space, are the bright silver lights of distant suns and galaxies. This can be more "divinity" for us if we need it, as it was obvious to our ancestors that these lights were gods. So many gods, too! Millions and billions and trillions of them.

The stars are mystery incarnate. The stars are the promise of infinity and the tease of intelligent alien life. The stars remind us of the Linear Spiral. To some, the Stars seem like they are the entrance to the Abyss, but they are far enough away to remain non-threatening.

Nonetheless the Stars are terrifying echoes of eternity and scale, far beyond human comprehension. But with their suggestion of infinity there is also the offer of everlasting life. After all, warm, light, active presence cannot stop being. Over and over and over again...

THE SATELLITE VIEW

The Satellite View is Truth. From here we see everything. We see the Sun, the Moon, the Stars, and we see the entire Landscape of Being wrapped up in the Earth beneath us, silently screaming through space as the Satellite maintains its electro-chemically propelled orbit far above the Mountain of Reason. All life that we know of – everything human – we see the whole thing contained in a small, delicate sphere. We see the fragile, transitory nature of it all. We see the futility of it all counterbalanced with the critical importance of it all. We see how fleeting and beautiful it all is.

The Satellite View is a manmade view because, like the satellite itself, truth is a manmade construct. The Satellite View reminds us that humanity is who defines humanity. And this reflects back onto the Self to remind us that the Self is who defines the Self.

One of the side effects of advances in technology has been to pull us away from our ancient and primal selves. By itself, this is not necessarily a bad thing. After all, our ancient and primal selves were far less civilized than we are today. And civilization is a good thing! So, while wearing shoes disconnected us from contact with the land and driving cars has disconnected us from our horses, these technologies have also brought us to even more advances in technology which have unified us in a global network. Technology has forced us to widen our view and consider other perspectives.

The Satellite View reminds us that human advances in technology are part of being human and that we must integrate this knowledge into our spirituality. We can embrace our spirituality *and* our technology. They are not mutually exclusive. In fact, to deny our technology is to deny part of who we have become as humans.

Part of the truth we are exposed to with the Satellite View is the truth of our own mortality. First, the Satellite cannot maintain its orbit forever. Second, we can see the Abyss and the Other Side from here and we know that all life must enter the great transformation we call "death."

THE ABYSS

The Abyss can also be synonymous with the Other Side, but more technically, the Abyss is the entrance *to* the Other Side.

The Abyss is a great whirlpool sucking everything back into the Scattering of All. It is like a black hole for the Self. The Abyss tears down everything that has been built up and brings it all back down the well of the Sea of Self past the Spirit-Consciousness, past the raw Awareness and Form we find in the Wilderness and deeper still to All, itself. This is warm, light, active presence again with "no Form."

Often, we hear talk about the terror of looking into the Abyss. Why is no Form scary? No Form is scary because once we achieve the state of no Form, we return to the Scattering and our egos are no longer around to tell us who we were or how to "come back." We can and will come back, but in an infinite cosmology, coming back from the Scattering is a matter of time and luck. We will certainly come back. Over and over and over again. But our ego desires to control the situation and formless warm, light, active presence is outside of our control. The Abyss is the gateway back into the pure chaos we originally came from. And pure chaos is scary. For anyone who has stared into the Abyss, the terror of going there is very real. It is clear from looking into the Abyss that if we enter here, we will "never" come back.

THE OTHER SIDE

If the Abyss is the entrance to the Other Side, and we can enter but "never" come back, what exactly is on the Other Side?

The Other Side is the great transformation. The Other Side is where we go after death.

So far, our science has yet to document what takes place on the Other Side.

There are many supernatural explanations for what happens to our Spirit-Consciousness after death. Most all of these involve the Spirit-Consciousness continuing to persist in some manner.

But supernatural explanations aside, there are also many logical and natural explanations for how it could be that our

Spirit-Consciousness may persist after death and still not come back to "this side."

One thing is certain: as warm, light, active presence, we cannot desist. Even if we are exhausted and wish for the "final sleep," in many real ways we cannot find it on the Other Side because as warm, light, active presence we cannot cease to exist. We learned this in in Chapter 1 at the very beginning when we saw how Not proves that All must be.

CHAPTER 16: THE SEARCH FOR SELF

CINEREO ASCENSUS (THE GRAY CLIMB)

In Chapter 1, we started with Not and from there we began to climb the cosmological ladder of Not. As we made our ascent, we saw how the Cosmology of Not aligned with the Cosmology of Self and how both of those cosmologies aligned with the cosmology of the universe. It is no real surprise to find such interconnectedness across these boundless cosmologies when we consider that each of us is a reflection of the universe we live in. Universes within the universe. Multiverses. The ascent from Not to the Shallows of the Sea of Self is called Cinereo Ascensus "the gray climb."

The "grayness" of the climb comes from the knowledge that there is no pure and perfect good and there is no pure and perfect evil. Just as there can be no up without down and no inside without outside, there can be no good without evil. Both must exist, therefore neither can exist without the other. As such, there are only shades of gray that run between these two conceptual extremes.

One can metaphorically perform all or part of this ascent at any time. A brief meditation on a small part of the ascent might be the equivalent of taking a deep spiritual breath and letting it out.

For example, I might close my eyes, imagine the warm, light, active present Scattering of All for a moment as the fundamental basis of reality. I can hear the buzzing hum of it. I feel the warmth, light, activity, and presence inside me, in the air around me and in the people and places around me. I realize that through this medium of All, we are all connected. The Unity of All…

This is the spiritual breathing in and out that I need for a quick reset. It is especially helpful to synchronize a deep physical breath in and out while mentally and spiritually breathing in and out with this thought exercise. I then open my eyes and carry on with my business of being in the world.

A full Cinereo Ascensus is a guided (or self-guided) ascent from Not to the Community Principle.

In this meditation (or contemplation), one should slowly step through the Cosmology of Not in one's mind, taking in the significance of each rung in the ladder and each jump point in between the rungs until the Community Principle is reached.

Cinereo Ascensus reminds us of what is most important in life. What is most important in life is being Who we are and What we are. Giving *Being* this kind of high honor is paying homage and respect to the value and power of life itself. We are showing awe and humble deference to this amazing gift of *Being*. In this way, Who and What I am is the most important thing in my universe. And as a complete reflection of *our* universe, when I show such deference and respect to my Self, I am conveying the same humility and awe to our universe.

The other significant aspects of the Who and the What of the Self are that the Who and the What of the Self are the truth of the Self. These parts of the Self are what remain regardless of what is thrown at us in the Landscape of Being.

I can lose my stamp collection, my money, or my home. I can lose my job, my partner, or my pet. I can even lose a limb or the ability to walk or talk. But no matter how much I lose in the Landscape of Being; I am still the *Who* and the *What* of the Self that was discovered in Cinereo Ascensus. These are the aspects of Self that cannot be taken from me no matter what. The *Who* and the *What* are the aspects of the Self that were forged into Form in the Scattering of All, then journeyed to and through the Landscape of Being; the very same aspects of the Self that will ultimately enter the Abyss and move on to the Other Side.

CINEREO MODO (THE GRAY WALK)

With all of its illusion, sham, heartbreak, disaster, pain, and misery, why should we even enter the Landscape of Being? Why not just get to the depths of Being in the Sea of Self and hang out there indefinitely?

We can't just remain at one level of Cinereo Ascensus because we are flesh and blood creatures and therefore we require sustenance, movement, and rest. We need to move around and do stuff. The Landscape of Being is illusory but it also isn't. Just like money, the Landscape of Being does not really exist. But also, just like money, we *must* interact with the Landscape of Being anyway.

The Landscape of Being is the world around us. It is the paradigm humanity's ancestors have constructed for us. It is the great machine that gives, takes, creates, and destroys. It is what Amos called, "the churn." Surely it is not what you or I would have designed[17] had we been given the project. But it is what we have.

While we cannot just choose one level of Cinereo Ascensus and stay there, we can – if we should want to – choose only one area of the Landscape of Being and just remain there indefinitely. However, this is not recommended.

In order to fully flesh out the Self and complete the inner journey, we need to embark on the trek across the Landscape of Being.

The journey across the Landscape of Being is called Cinereo Modo (the gray walk). Just like with the Ascensus, the "grayness" of the walk comes from the knowledge that there is no source of pure good or pure evil in reality. There are only shades of gray that run between these two conceptual extremes thus the path we walk is a gray path.

THE AFTER

This book has presented a brief overview of the Cosmology of Not along with an introduction to the Landscape of Being. Both of these sweeping concepts, when combined, are excellent cornerstones to a strong foundation which can be used in the search for Self.

There was a time, many moons ago, I worked the night shift at a gas station. One morning during shift change, one of my coworkers shared a saying with me that his father had passed down to him: "A task begun is a task half done."

---

[17] From the Dark Side of the Moon: "God only knows, it's not what we would choose... to do..."

I mulled that over for several days before accepting it as sound advice. Ever since, I have found it to be quite true.

The search for Self (aka. the Inner Journey) is a nebulous idea which is difficult to define and even more difficult to undertake. There are thousands of guides available to the one who is seeking guidance. However, the truth of the matter is that nobody knows how to get to the destination of the Inner Journey until they get there. And then, they can only know how they made their own journey.

Once we arrive, we realize we've arrived, but what each of us finds there is different.

And when we've found our innermost Self and feel "we have arrived," we find that *what* we have arrived *at,* is a new beginning.

Whether you have just started your journey, or you have already arrived, something we all share in common is the purpose of life, which is *being*.

I would like to highlight one more truth which is often easy for us to overlook. It is another way of saying "the purpose of life is to be." In a final bout of celestial irony, the journey itself is actually the destination.

☙ Begin ❧

www.ingramcontent.com/pod-product-compliance
Lightning Source LLC
Chambersburg PA
CBHW071008040426

42443CB00007B/726